"YOUR OLD S...
HA...

ALDERSHOT
HISTORY TOUR

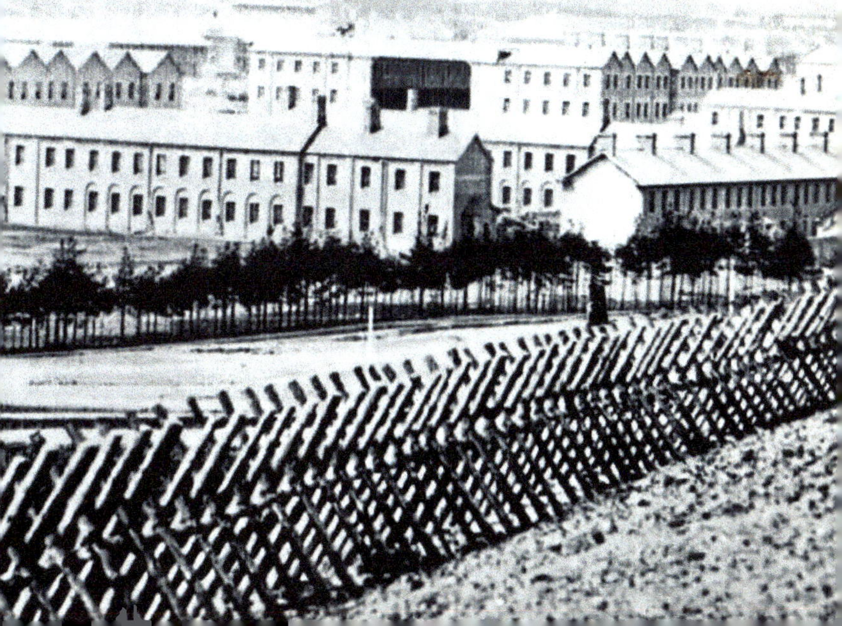

First published 2016

Amberley Publishing
The Hill, Stroud,
Gloucestershire, GL5 4EP
www.amberley-books.com

Copyright © Paul H. Vickers, 2016
Map contains Ordnance Survey data
© Crown copyright and database right
[2016]

The right of Paul H. Vickers to
be identified as the Author of this work
has been asserted in accordance with
the Copyrights, Designs and Patents
Act 1988.

ISBN 978 1 4456 6425 5 (print)
ISBN 978 1 4456 6426 2 (ebook)

All rights reserved. No part of this book
may be reprinted or reproduced or
utilised in any form or by any electronic,
mechanical or other means, now
known or hereafter invented, including
photocopying and recording, or in any
information storage or retrieval system,
without the permission in writing from
the Publishers.

British Library Cataloguing in
Publication Data.
A catalogue record for this book is
available from the British Library.

Typesetting by Amberley Publishing.
Printed in Great Britain.

INTRODUCTION

Aldershot has a rich heritage. Since the Army Camp was founded in 1854 the original small village has grown into a modern borough, the development of the civilian town inextricably linked to the presence of the military. Today the army garrison is still of major importance, but the balance has changed. At its height the garrison was home to some 17,500 soldiers, and the building of the camp led to a new Victorian town centre being built on fields west of the old village. Today there are around 4,800 soldiers, and the land occupied by the garrison has shrunk. The first areas to be given up were the cavalry barracks in the south of the camp, and in the twenty-first century much of old South Camp has been handed over for civilian development. Patterns of trade, business and employment in Aldershot have changed as the town has diversified.

This historical tour begins in the area of the old Aldershot village (Nos 1–6), before moving up the High Street, with a short diversion to the Redan (No. 7). We then move into the area of the great Army Camp (Nos 8–31) to see some of Aldershot's military heritage and how civilian development has now taken over parts of the original Army garrison. The tour then explores the Victorian town centre (Nos 32–45).

The full tour is 7.25 miles, but it could easily be done in three parts – village, garrison and town. Alternatively, for a shorter route you could go directly from St Andrew's Church (No. 17) to the Officers' Club (No. 21), leaving out Nos 18–20, which saves 1.5 miles. If you do this, a separate visit to the Aldershot Military Museum (No. 19) is strongly recommended, where there is much to see about Aldershot's military and civilian history.

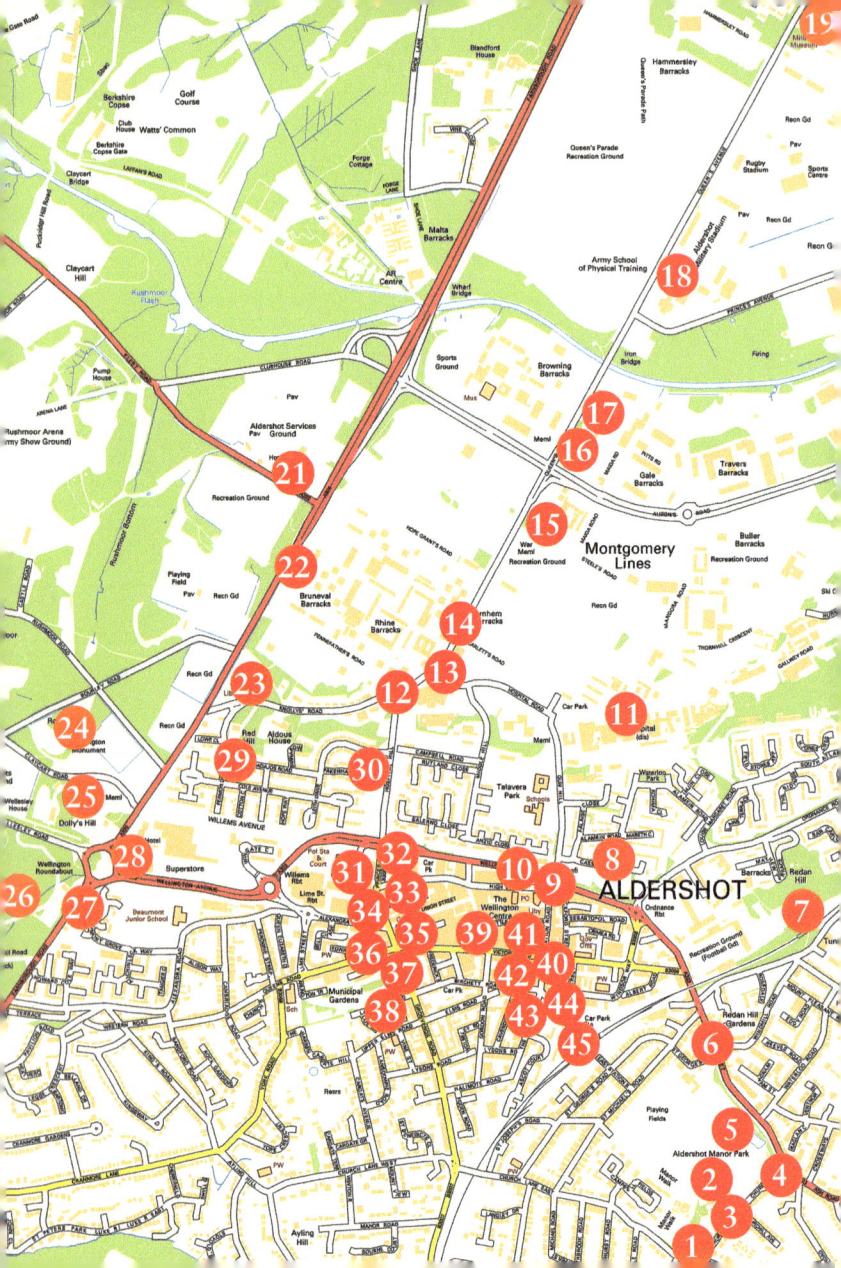

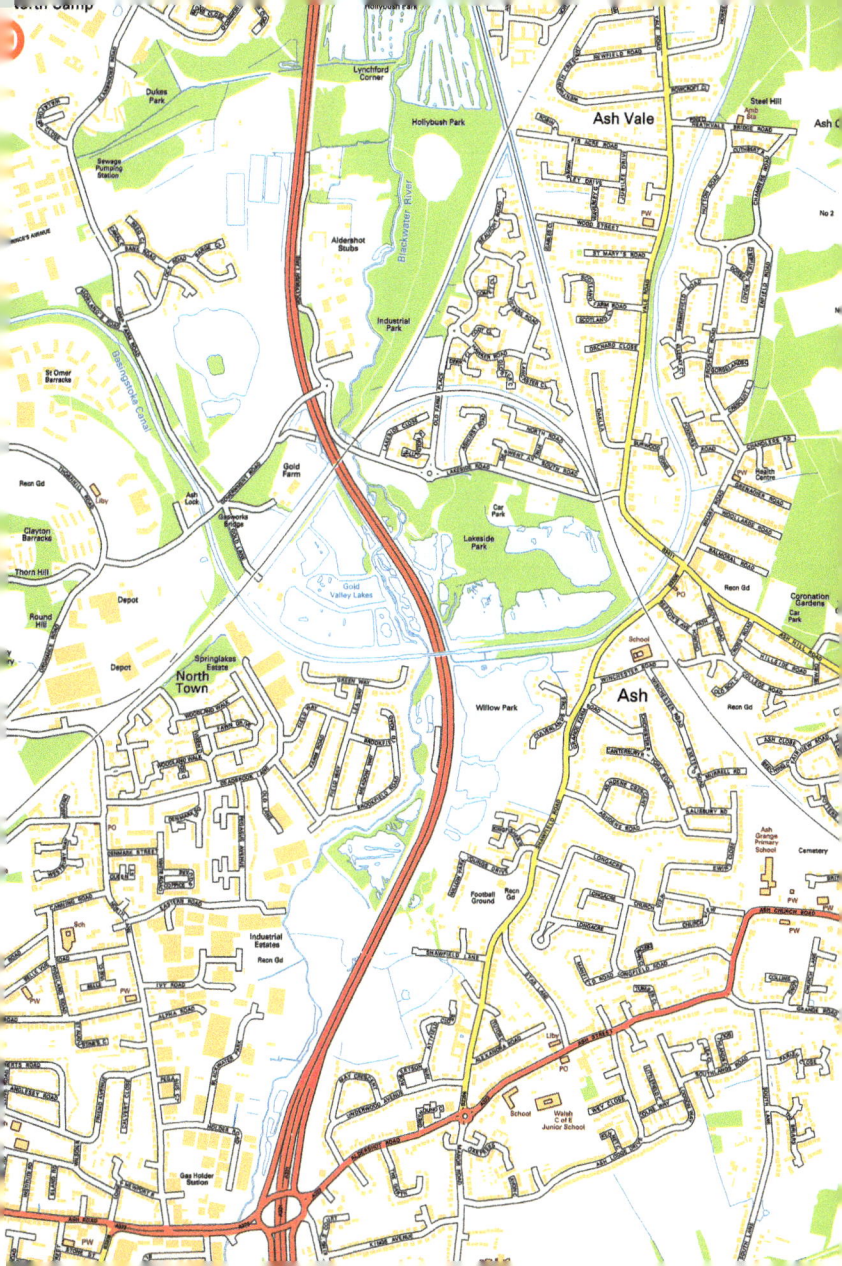

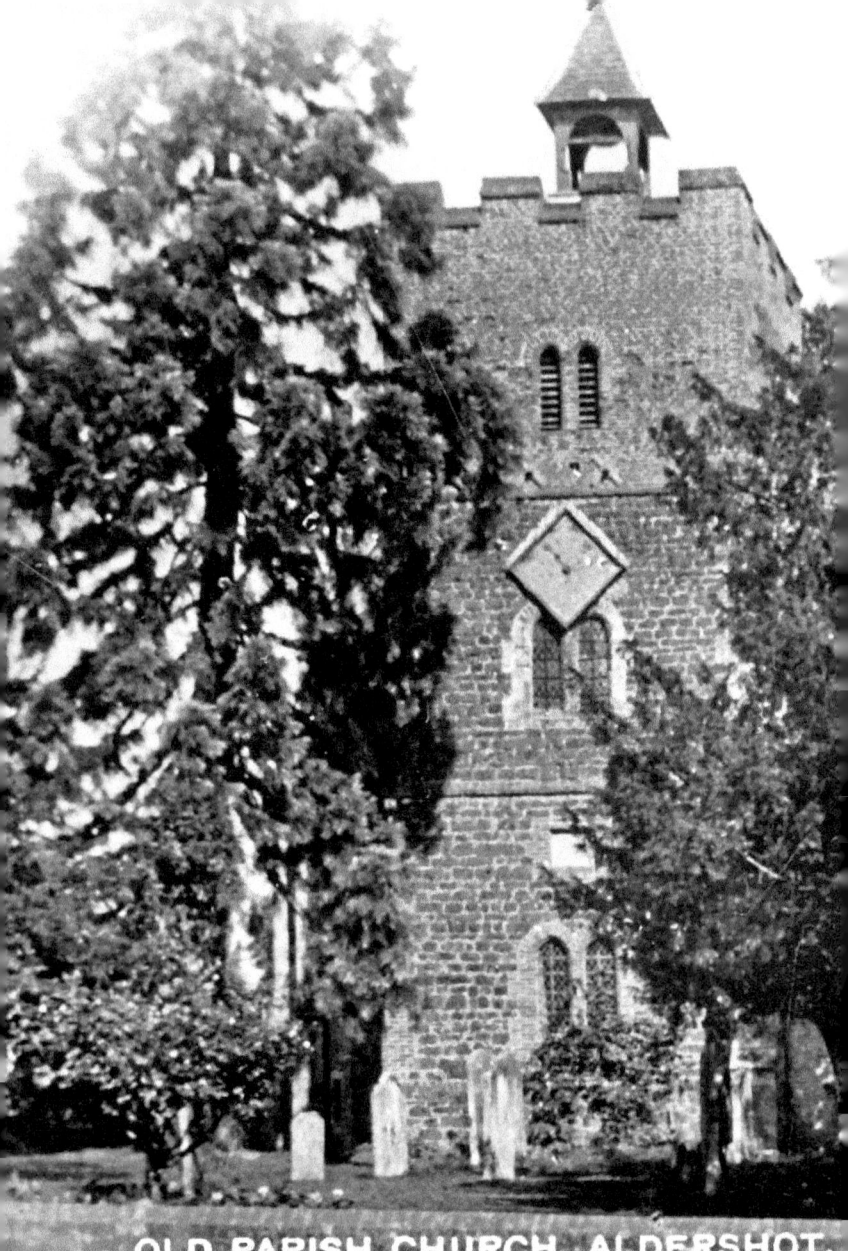
OLD PARISH CHURCH, ALDERSHOT.

1. THE ANCIENT PARISH CHURCH OF ST MICHAEL THE ARCHANGEL

The parish church dates from the twelfth century, with the oldest part of the church now forming the Lady Chapel. The brick tower was built around 1600, with the clock and turret bell installed in 1799. After the arrival of the Army, the church was extended in 1865 and again in 1911 to cope with the growing congregation. Since then it has changed very little.

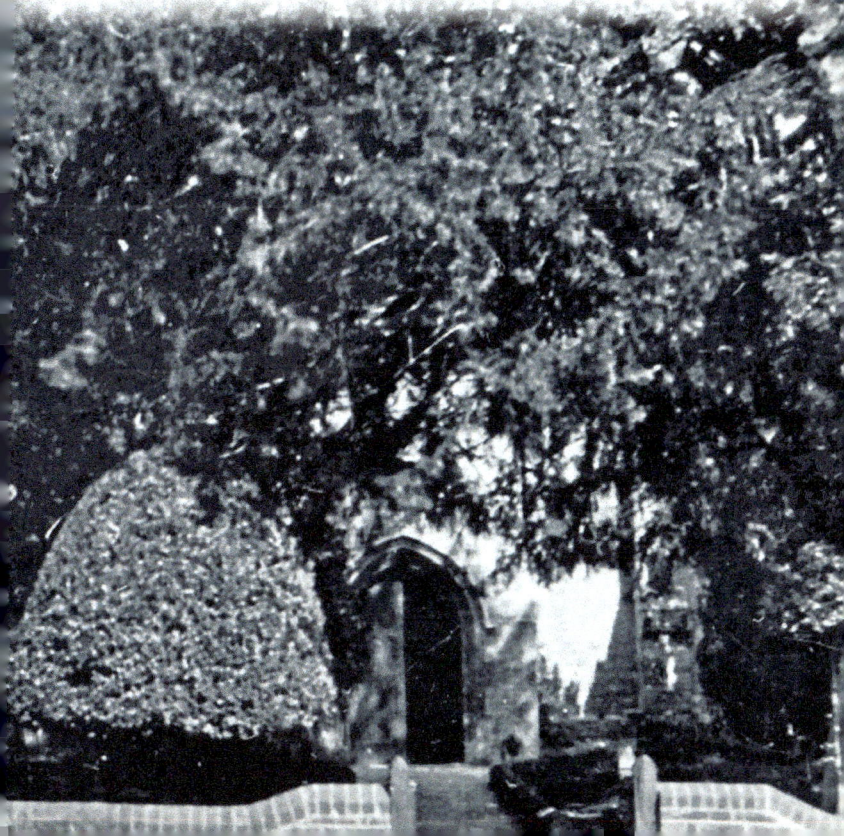

2. ALDERSHOT MANOR

Seen through the trees in this photograph from around 1930 is the Manor House, built in 1670 by the Tichbourne family to replace an older building in Aldershot Park. Although it has undergone numerous external and internal alterations over the years, the building is still in fine condition and is used today as offices.

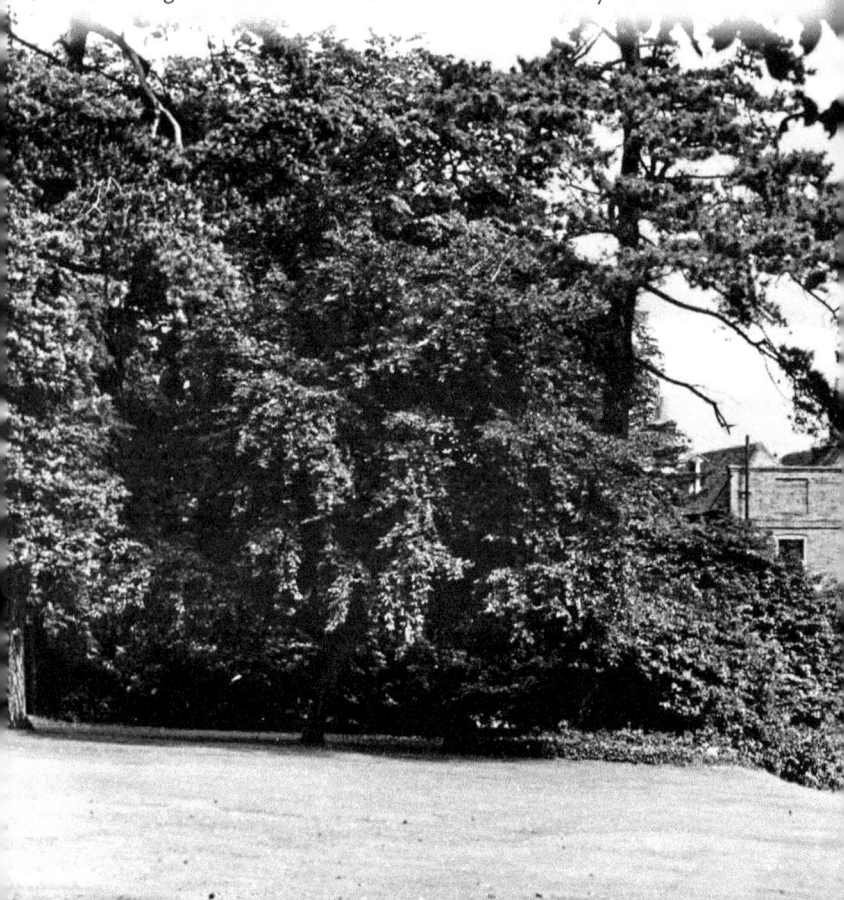

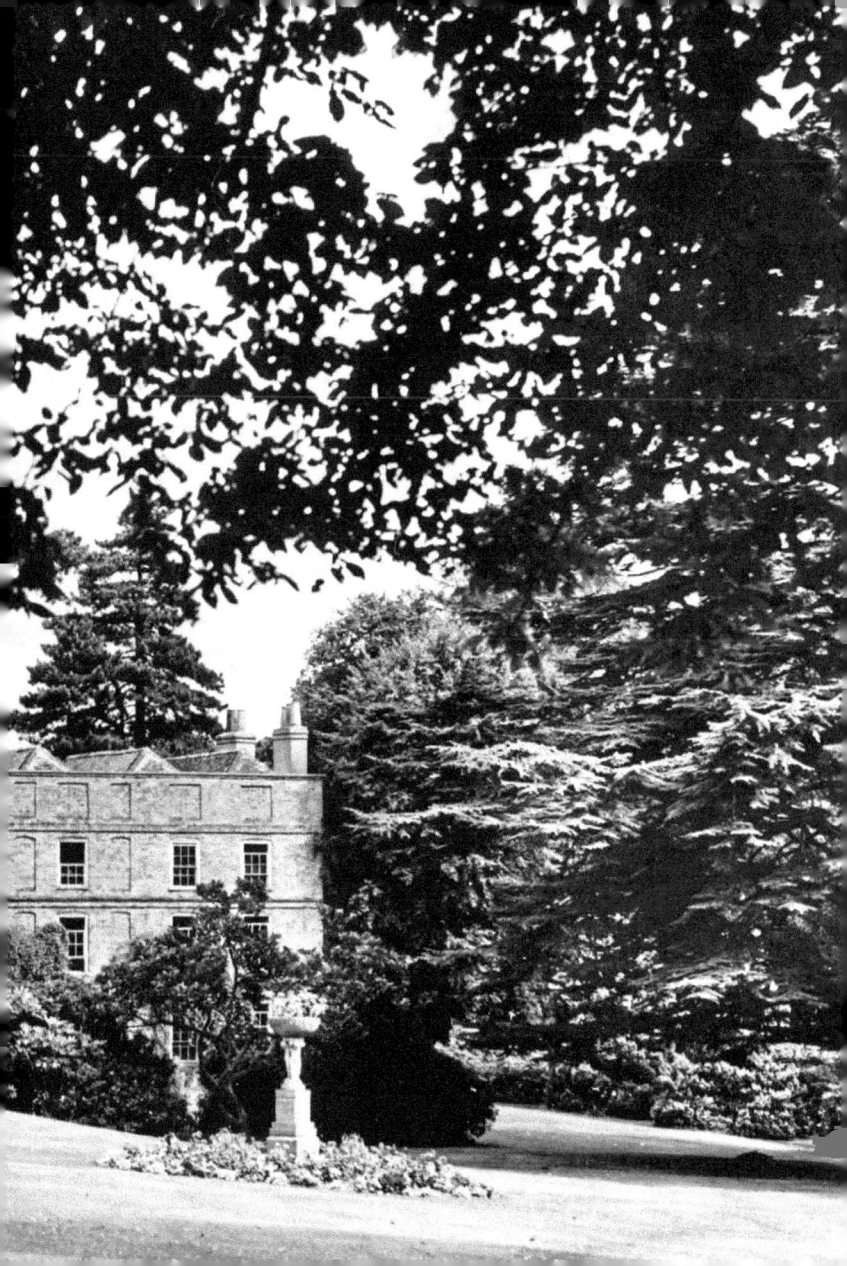

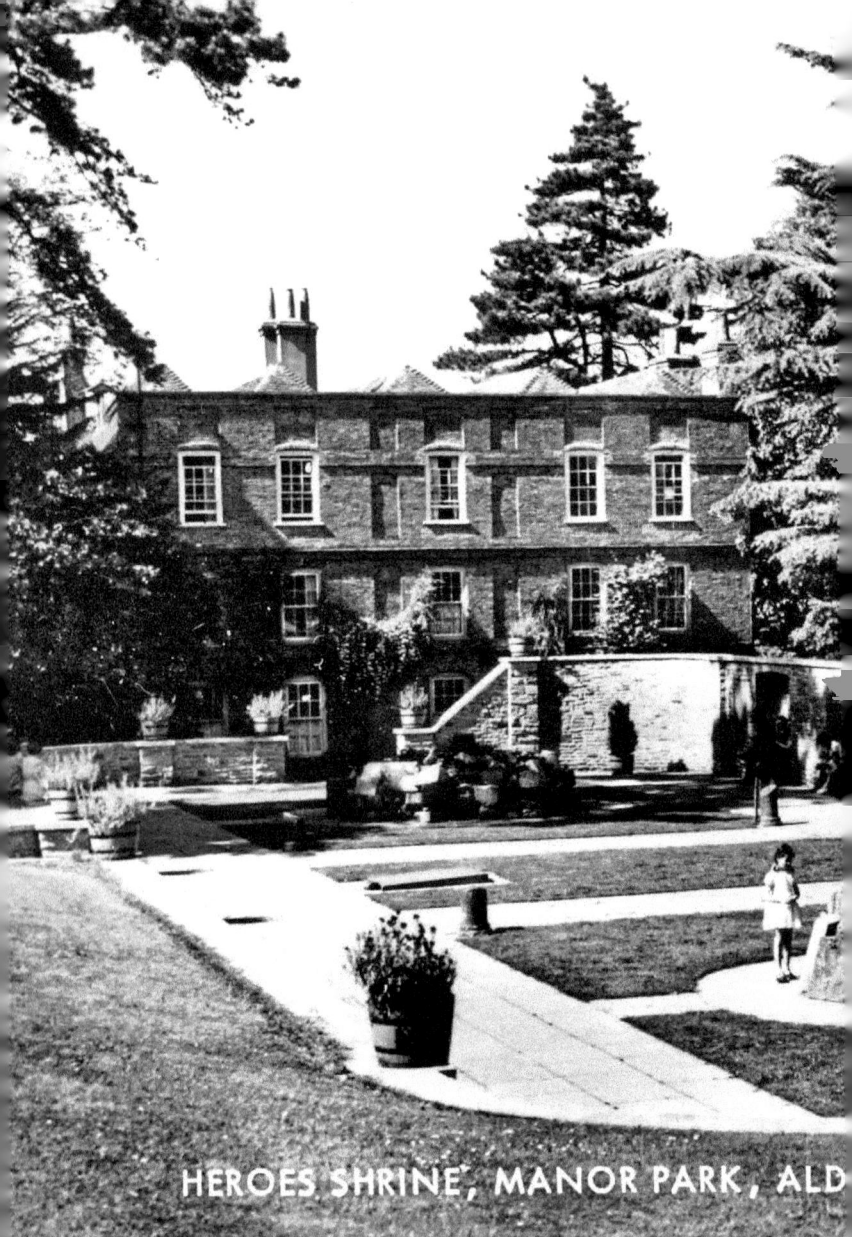

3. THE HEROES SHRINE

This national memorial to those killed during the Battle of Britain and by other enemy bombing in the Second World War was unveiled by the Duchess of Gloucester on 5 May 1950. It contains stones from thirty-four cities that suffered the most severe bombing, and the central sculpture is *Christ Stilling the Storm* by Josephina de Vasconcellos. In the 1990s the stones were repositioned to the present layout, but the original rockeries are shown in this photograph from around 1955.

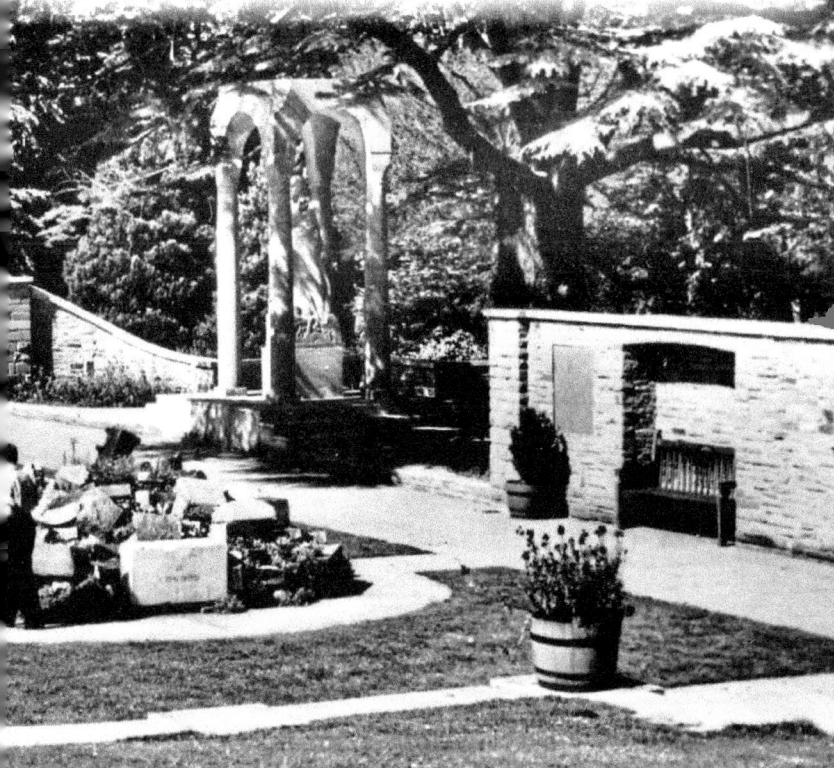

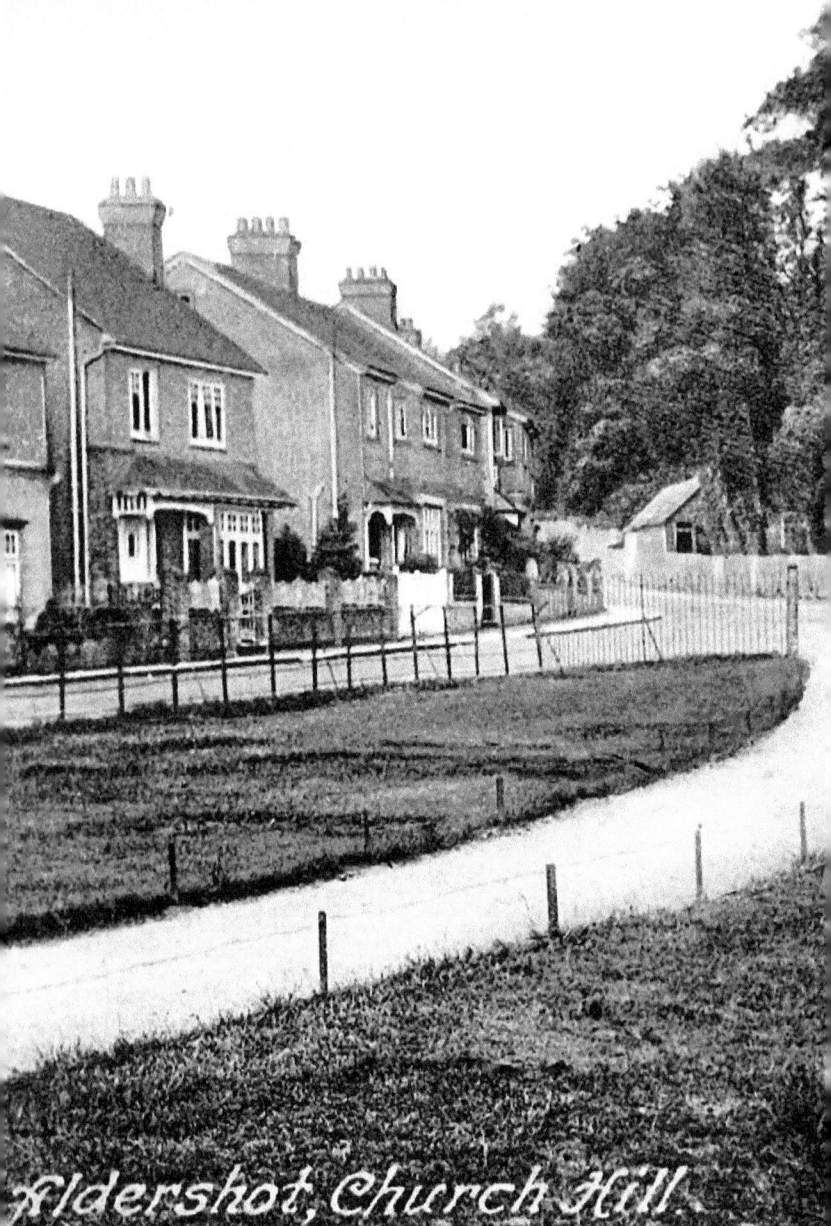

4. ALDERSHOT VILLAGE GREEN

Before 1853 Aldershot was a small village, with most of its buildings within a triangle formed by the parish church, the Red Lion inn, and the Beehive public house. The small patch of grass and flowers at the bottom of Church Hill marks the site of the village green. This photo dates from *c.* 1924 and is looking up Church Hill, with the Manor Park lodge on the right.

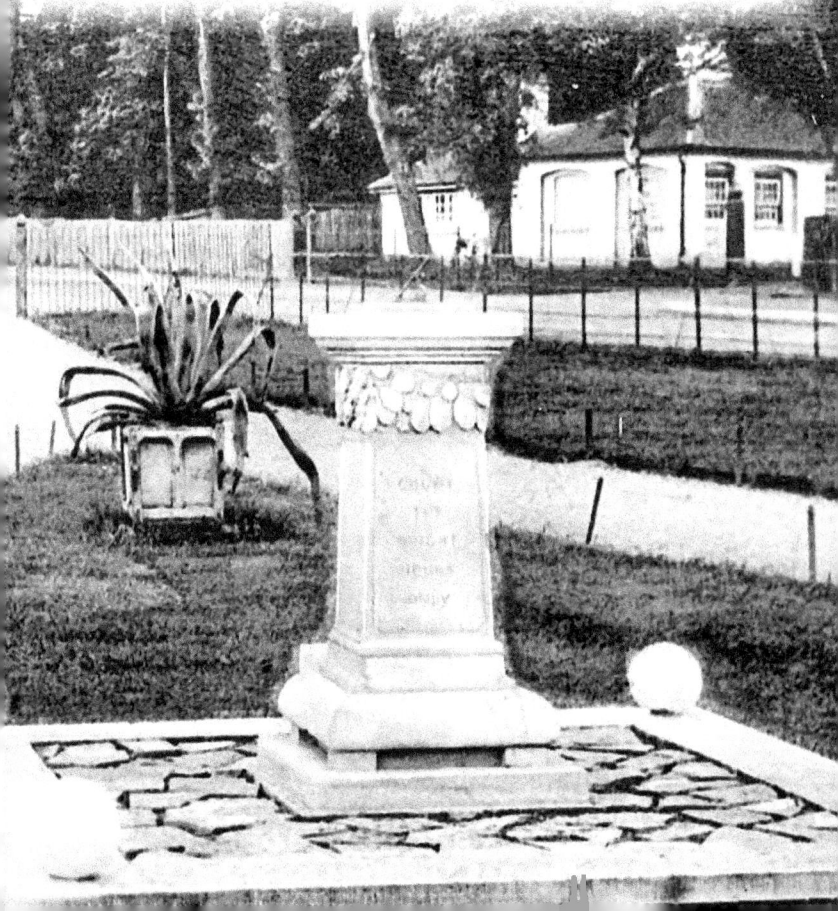

5. MANOR PARK

The grounds of the old Aldershot Manor were purchased by the council in 1919 and given to the people as a public park. The photograph, dating from around 1955, shows the lake by the High Street, and across the other side of the road is the Pavilion cinema, built in 1926. The peaceful scene around the lake remains, but the Pavilion was demolished in 1956 and an office block now stands in its place.

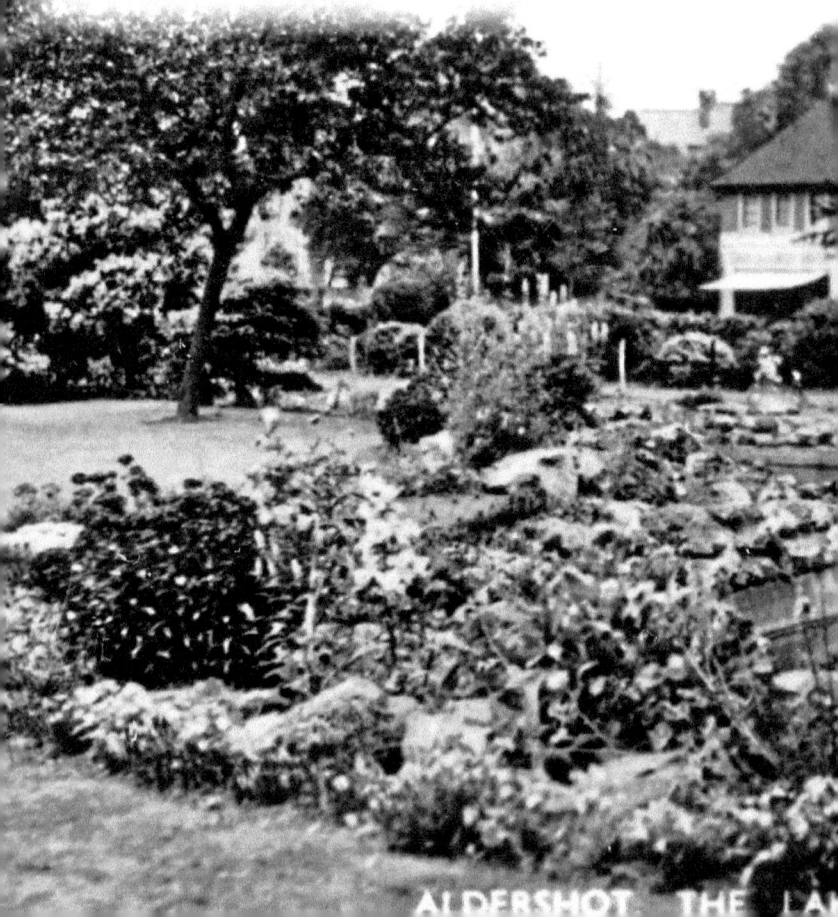

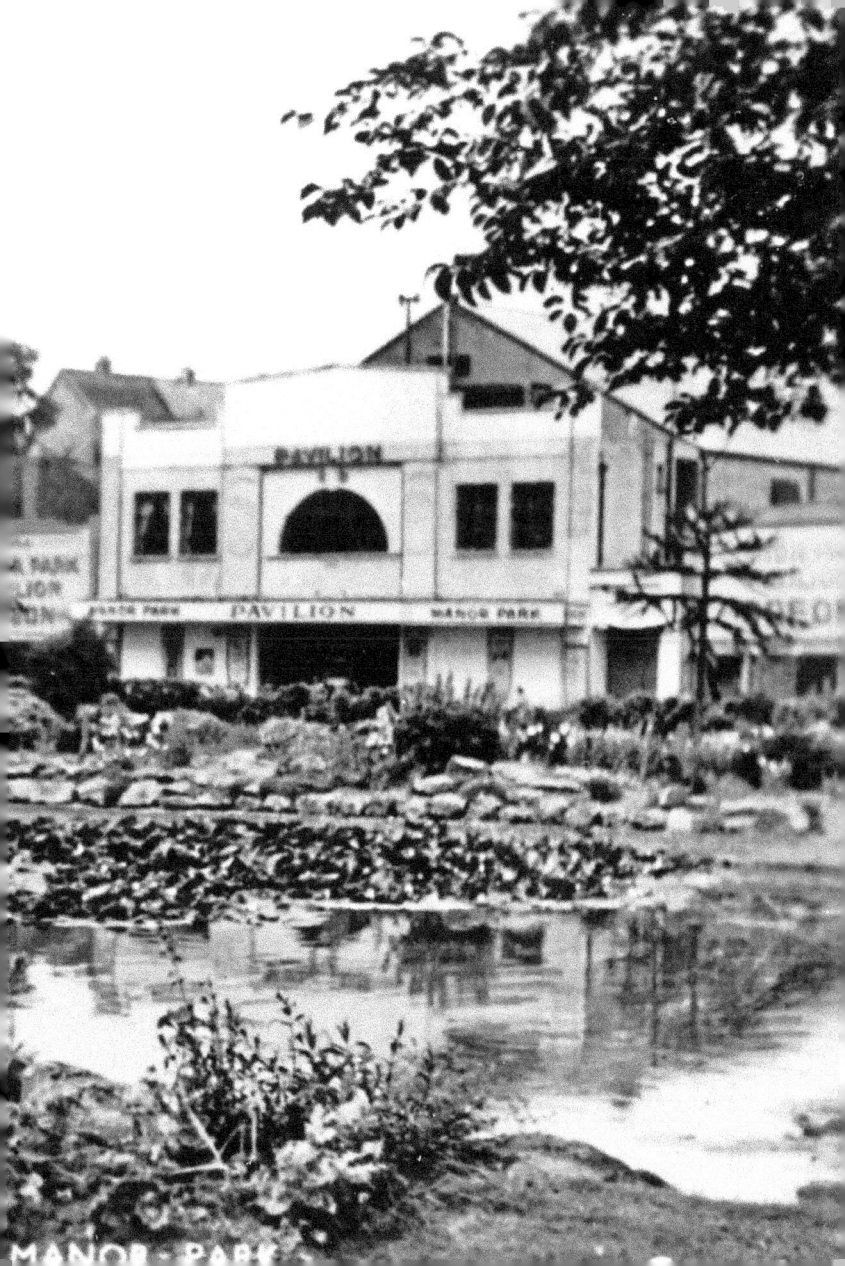

6. HIGH STREET FROM THE BEEHIVE

This view of the lower High Street from the 1920s looks past the line of shops to the railway bridge at the bottom of Redan Hill. On the right is the corner of the Beehive pub, one of the original pubs of Aldershot village, although it was rebuilt at some point between 1855 and 1871. The view has changed little today.

Turn right just before the railway bridge and go up Redan Road to the top of the hill for the next stop on the tour.

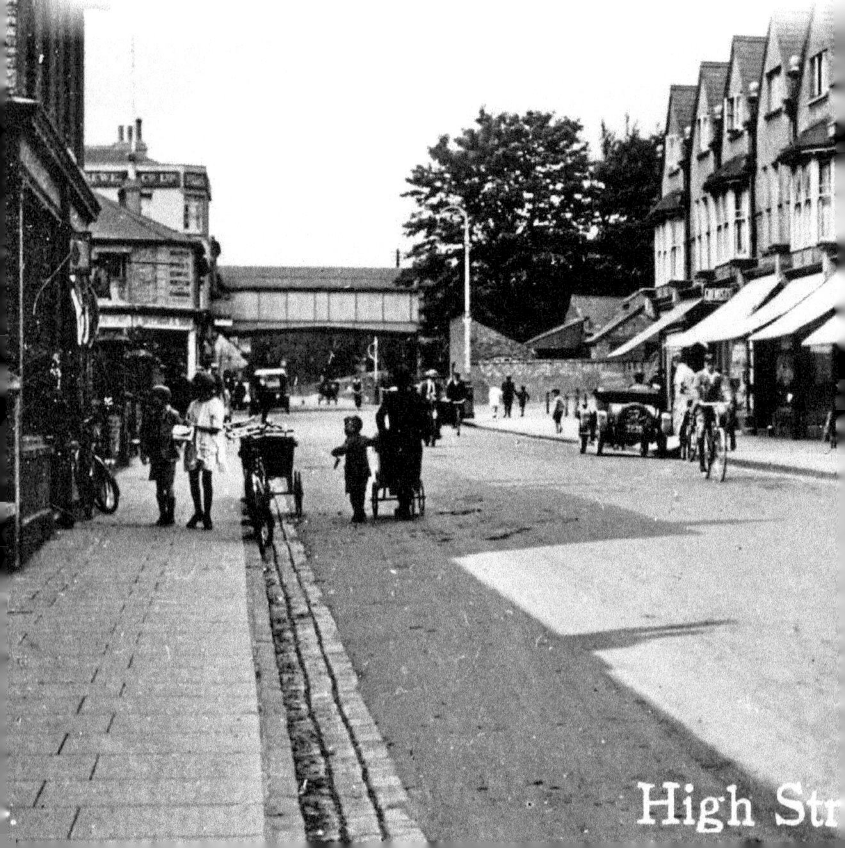

High Str

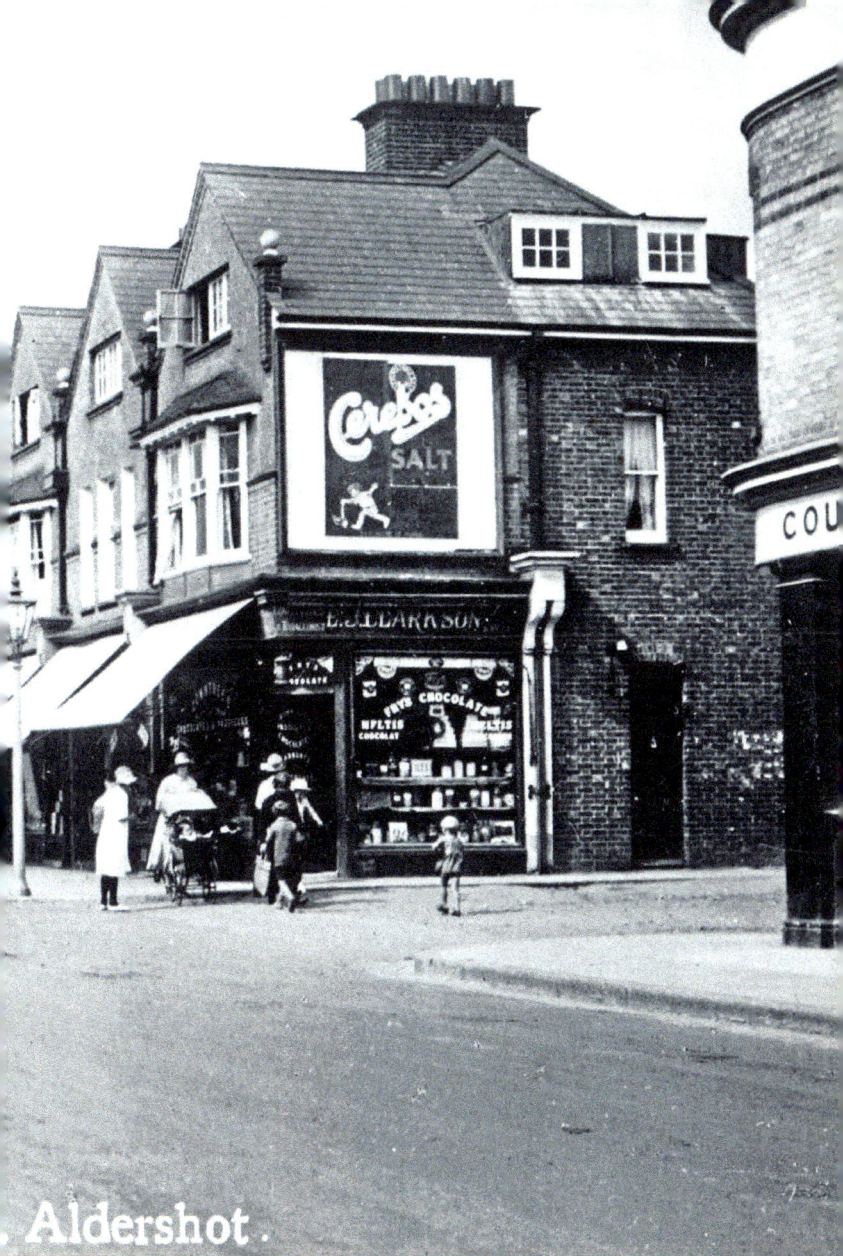

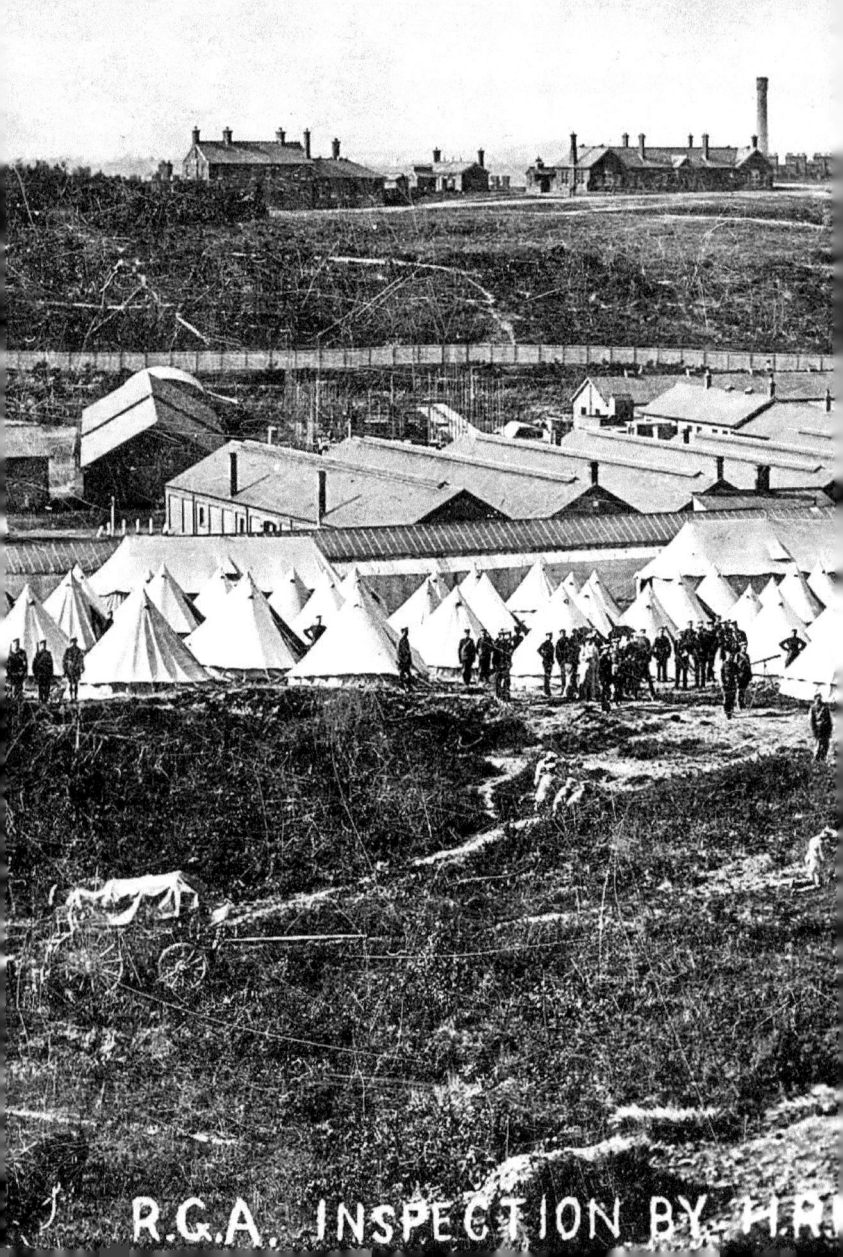

7. THE REDAN

The Redan fort was built in the 1850s to defend the camp from the south-east. This historic photograph is an inspection of the battery in 1906 by the Prince of Wales (later George V), and shows the view over the army's huge Field Stores and across to Peaked Hill. Unfortunately, the hill is now so thickly wooded that these views are lost. Parts of the Redan were restored by Rushmoor Council in 1990, with further work in 2015.

Retrace your steps back down Redan Road and continue under the railway bridge along High Street.

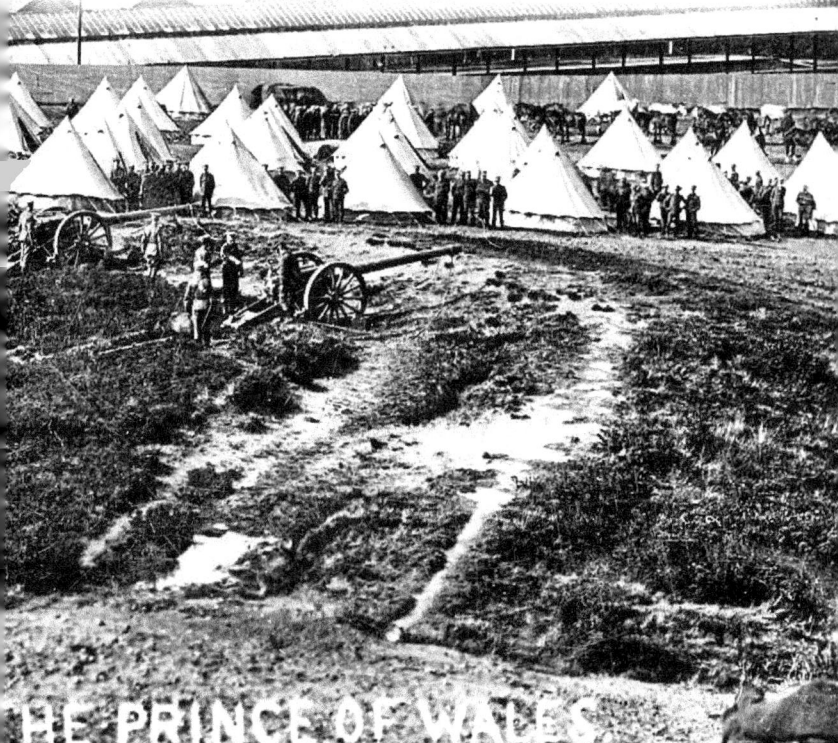

8. ROYAL ARTILLERY BARRACKS

The first permanent barracks were built between 1856 and 1859 and included two artillery barracks – one for foot and the other for horse artillery. Renamed in 1898 as Waterloo Barracks East and West, they were demolished in 1958/59 and replaced by army married quarters, which are still in use today. This photograph from 1883 shows the Royal Horse Artillery barracks officers' mess on the right and one of the blocks of troops' accommodations and stables on the left.

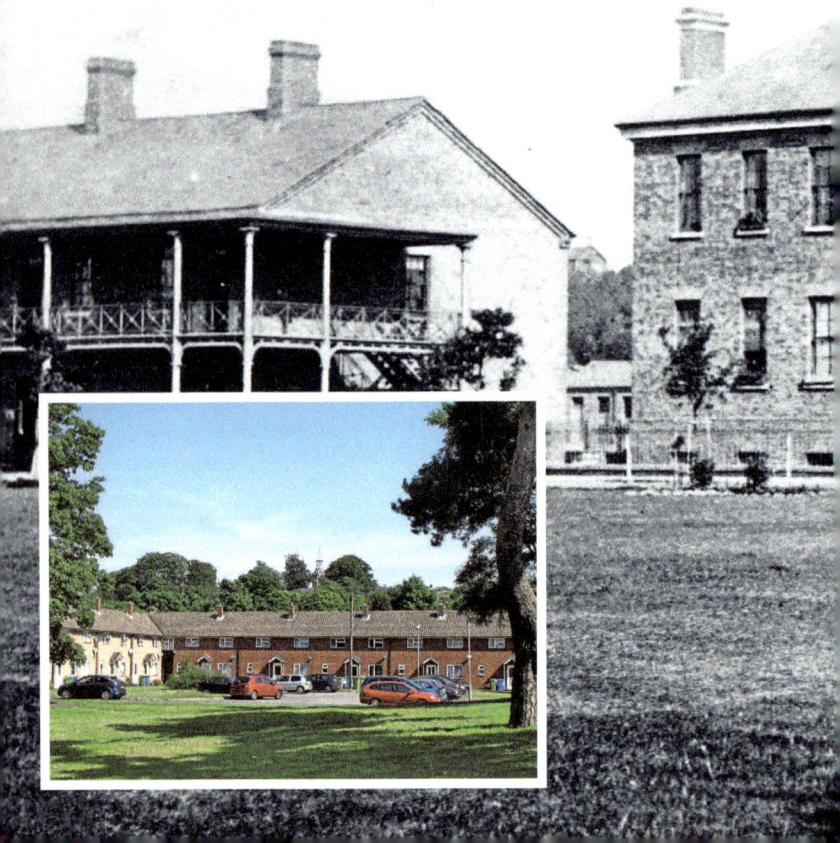

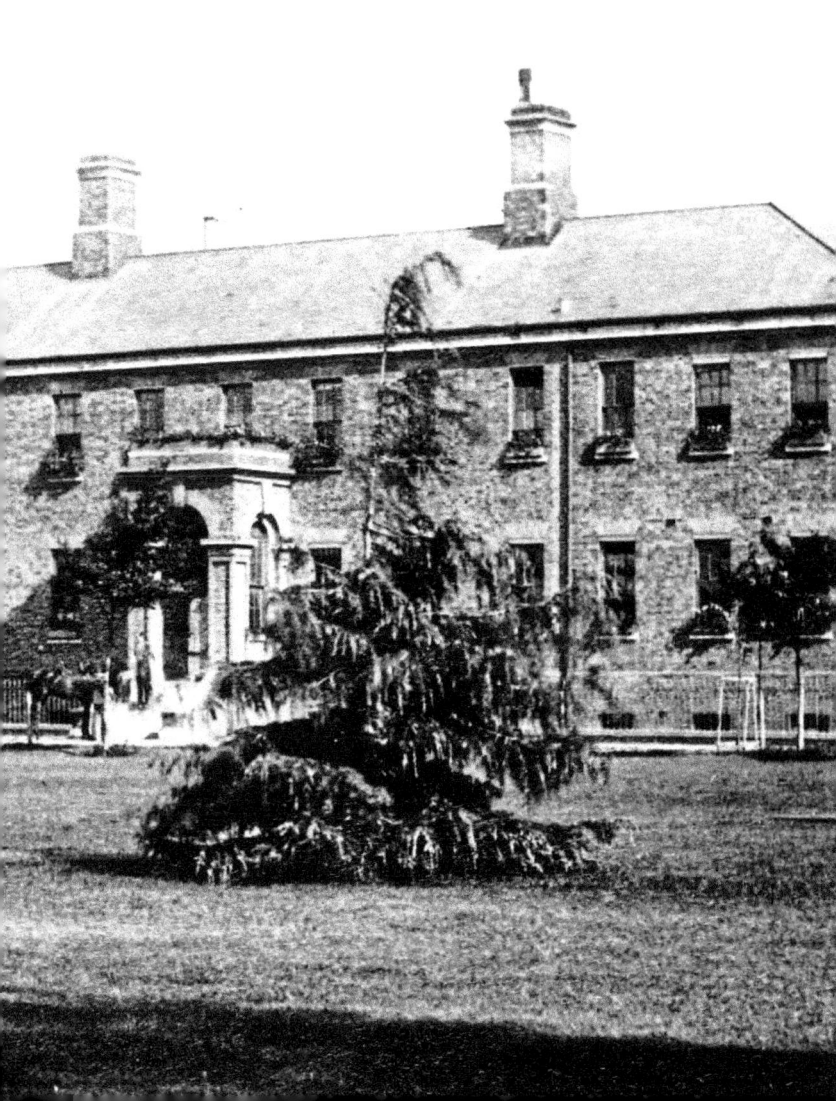

9. THE NAAFI ROUNDABOUT

This photograph was taken around 1950, looking from Station Road to the large NAAFI Club, which was opened in 1948 and built on the site of the old guardroom of Waterloo Barracks West. On the right is the Royal Exchange Hotel, which dates from 1873. The Royal Exchange closed in 2001 and was converted into flats. The NAAFI Club closed in 1971 and was demolished in the 1980s. A Burger King is on the site today.

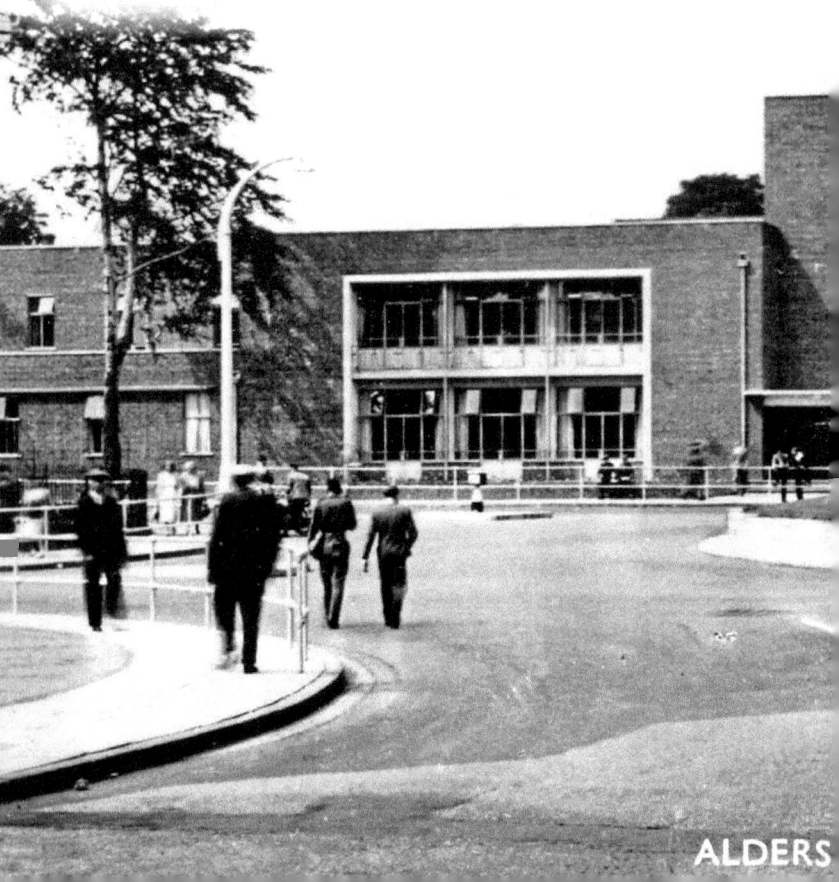

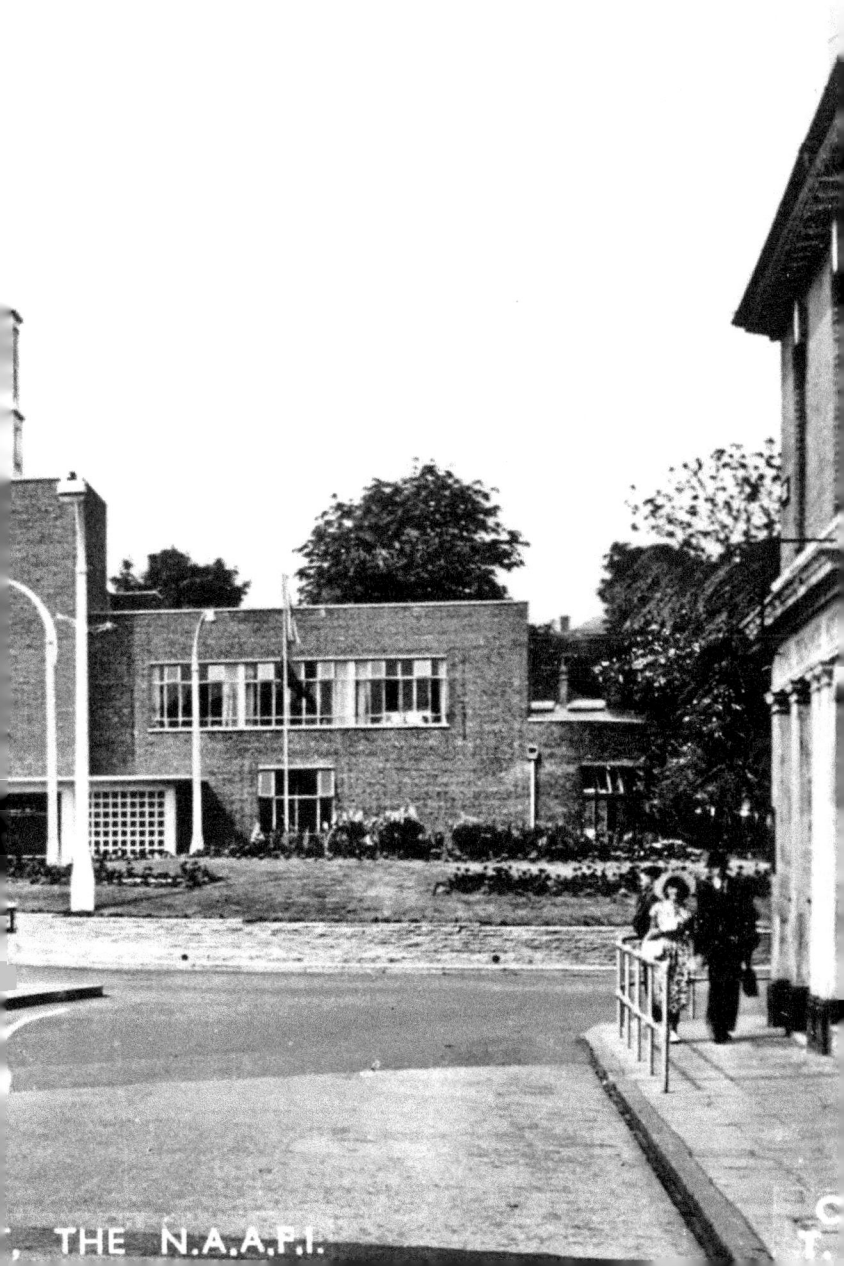
THE N.A.A.P.I.

10. WELLINGTON AVENUE

It is difficult today to appreciate how open Aldershot was in the early days of the camp. This photograph from 1870 shows the view looking west along what would become Wellington Avenue. On the right are the Artillery Barracks, then the Infantry Barracks, and the Garrison Church is clearly visible on the horizon. Today, the open spaces are filled with buildings and trees, but the church spire can still be seen in the distance.

From the NAAFI Roundabout, walk up Gun Hill to Hospital Road.

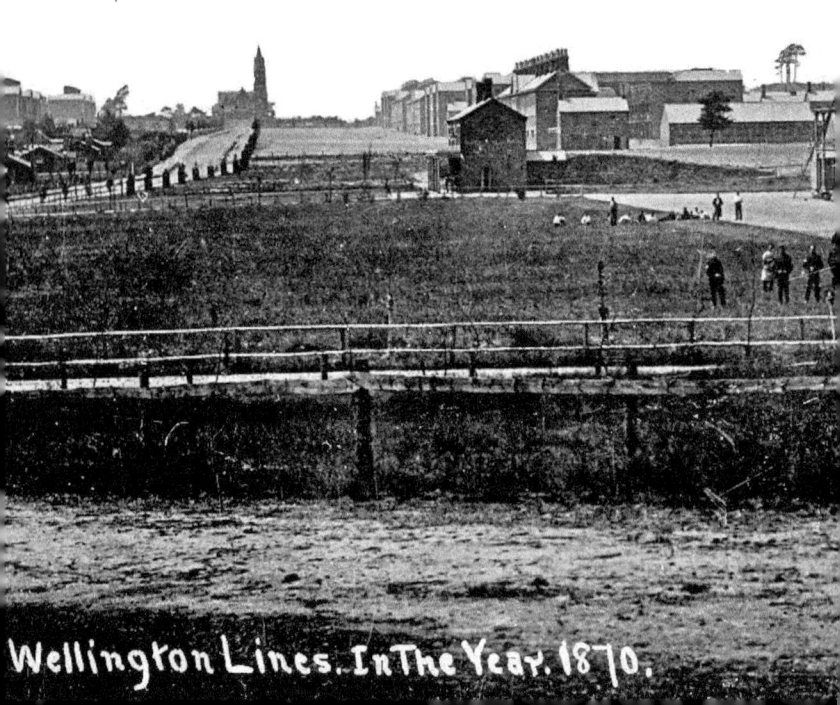

Wellington Lines. In The Year. 1870.

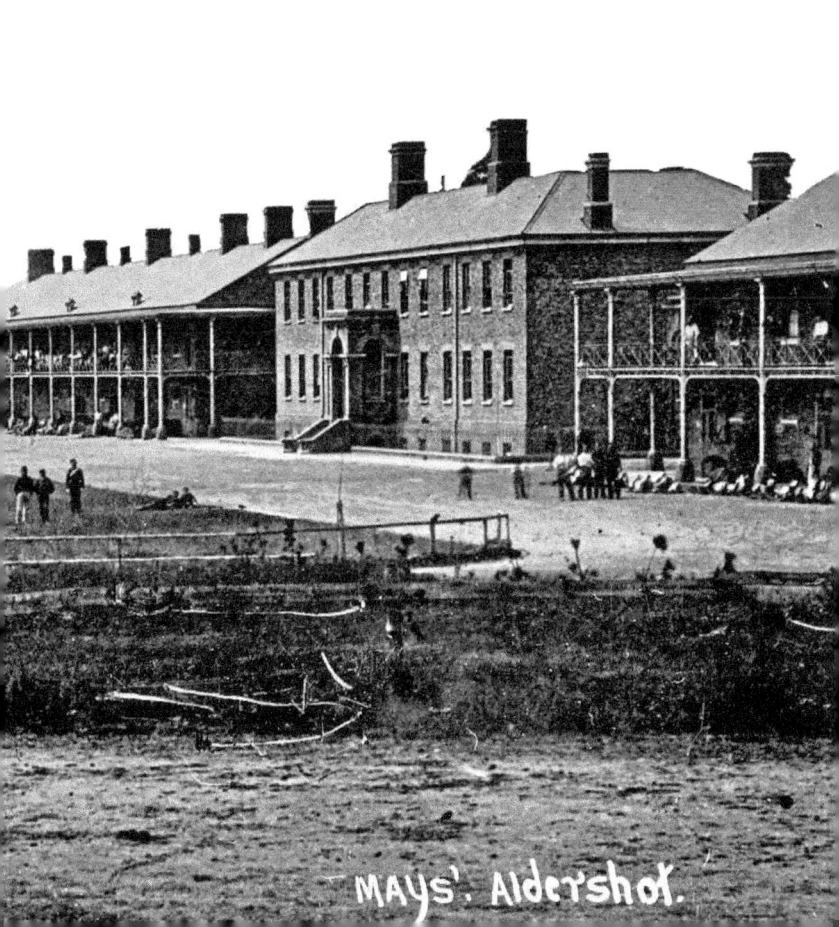

11. THE CAMBRIDGE HOSPITAL

Named after the Duke of Cambridge, commander in chief of the army, the Cambridge Military Hospital opened in 1879. The clock tower is 109 feet high, and the dials of the clock are 8 feet in diameter. The Cambridge closed in 1996 and military patients are now treated at Frimley Park NHS hospital. At the time of writing (2016), the building is being redeveloped for civilian residential apartments, so access is restricted during the building work, but Hospital Road will be open when the work is finished.

Return (west) along Hospital Road and continue to the junction with Queen's Avenue, then turn left to the top of Hospital Hill.

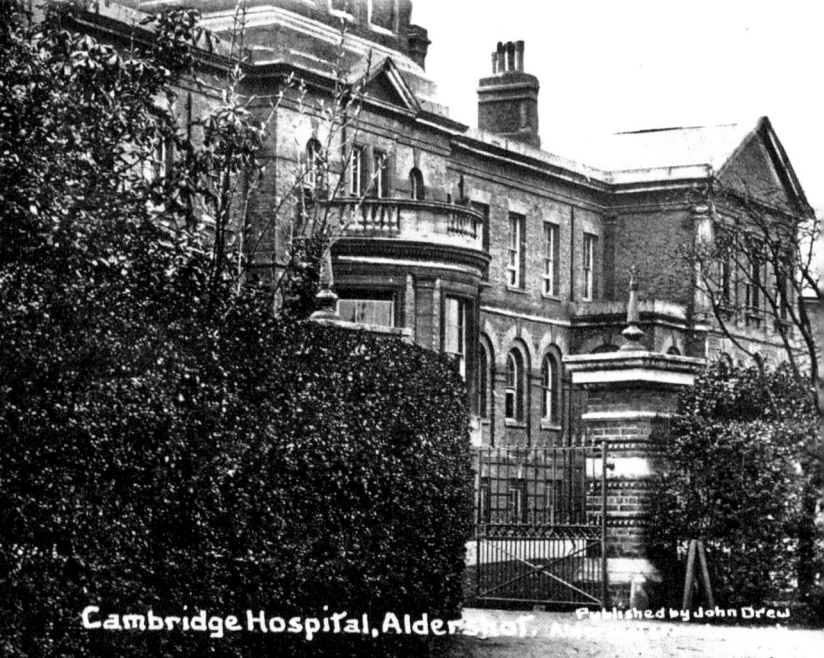

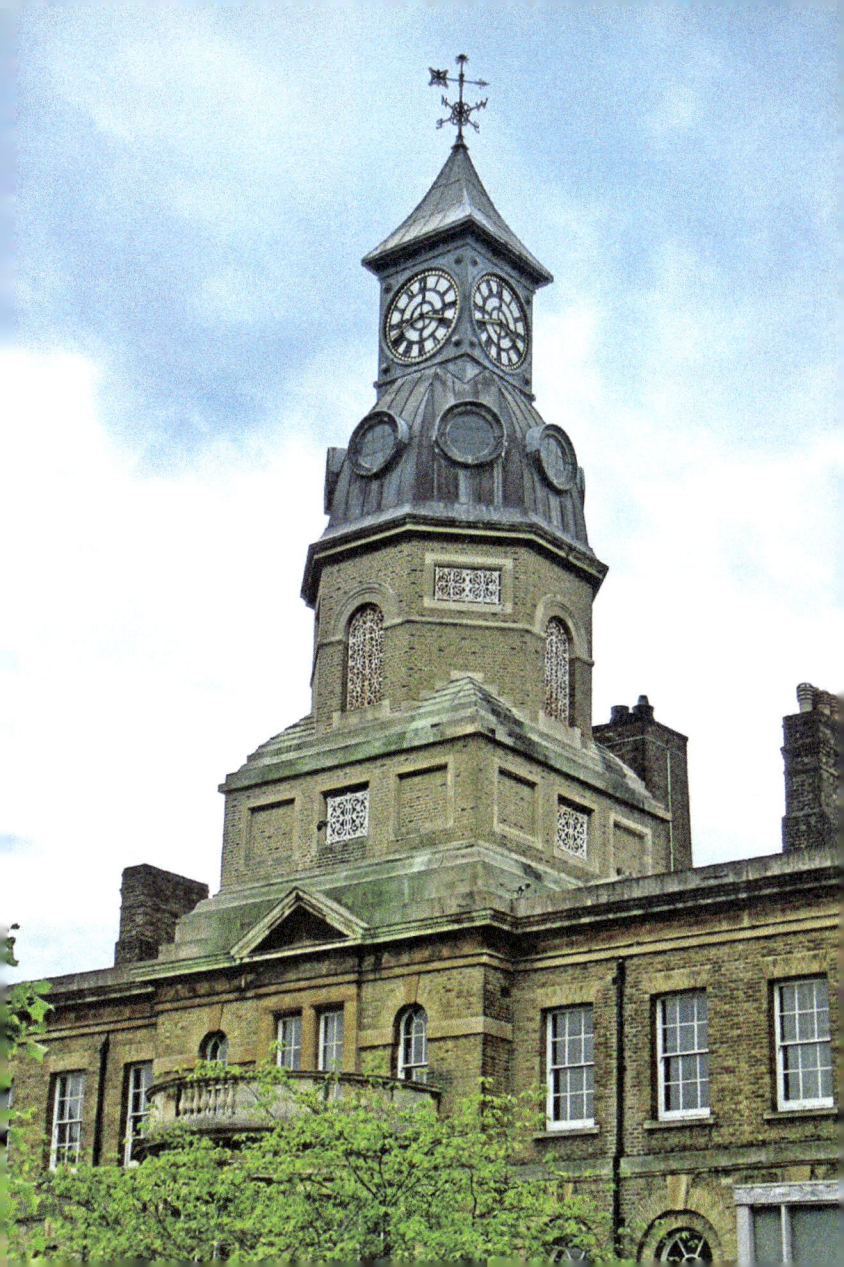

12. HOSPITAL HILL

The road takes its name from the original army hospital in Union Building, which is behind the trees on the right in the picture. The memorial on the mound in the right foreground is to the men of 2nd Division who fell in the First World War and was unveiled on 1 December 1923. There is little change between the views in this photo from 1949 with that of today.

Turn back north and walk along Queen's Avenue.

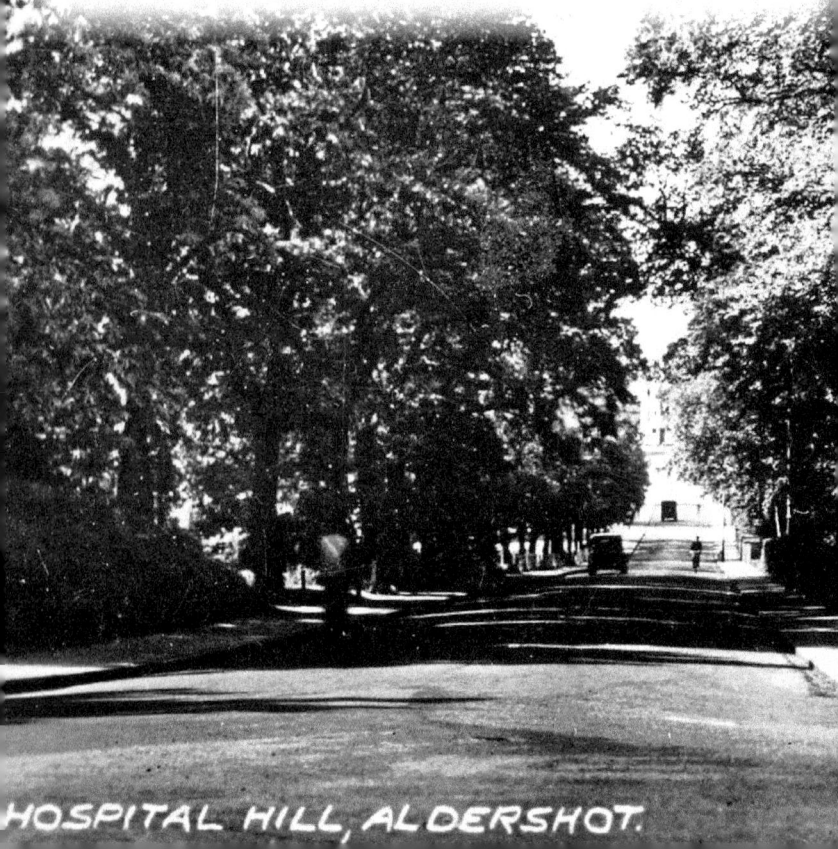

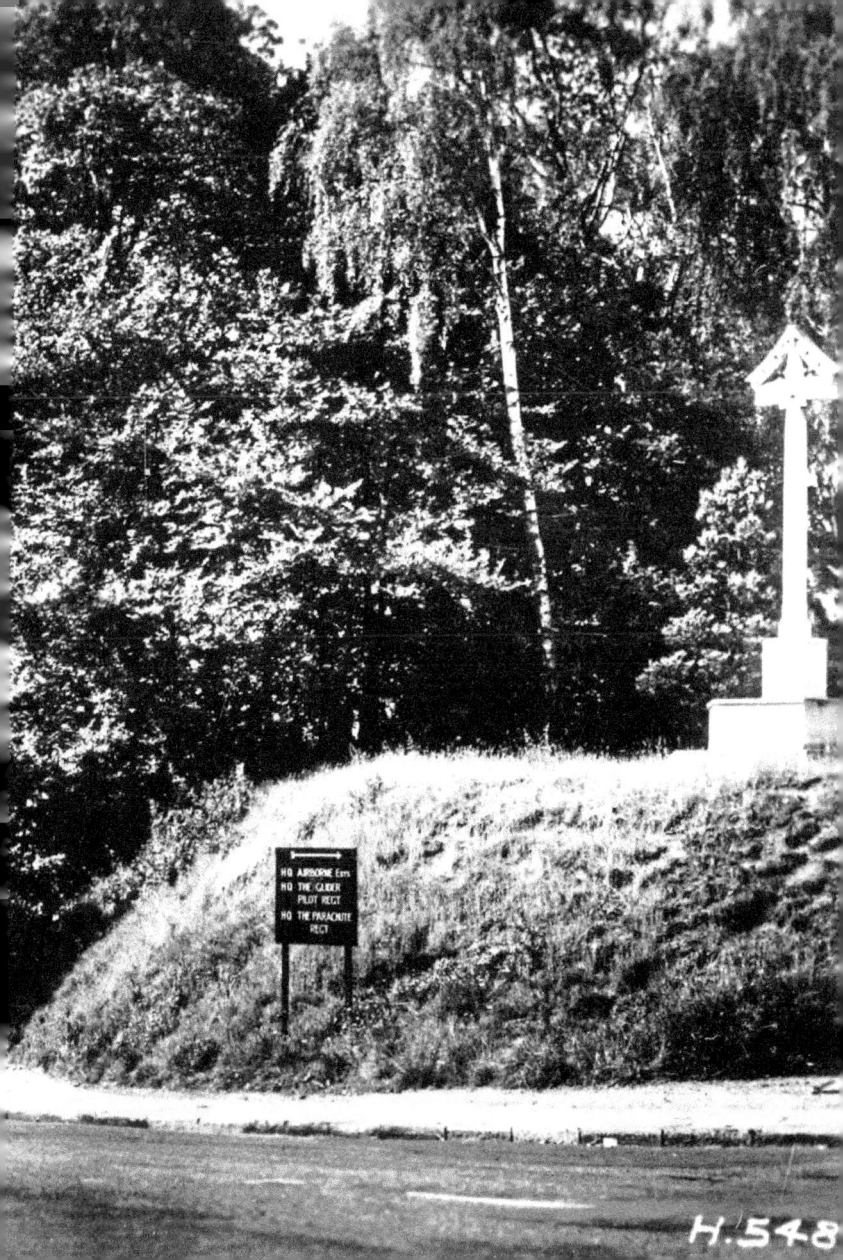

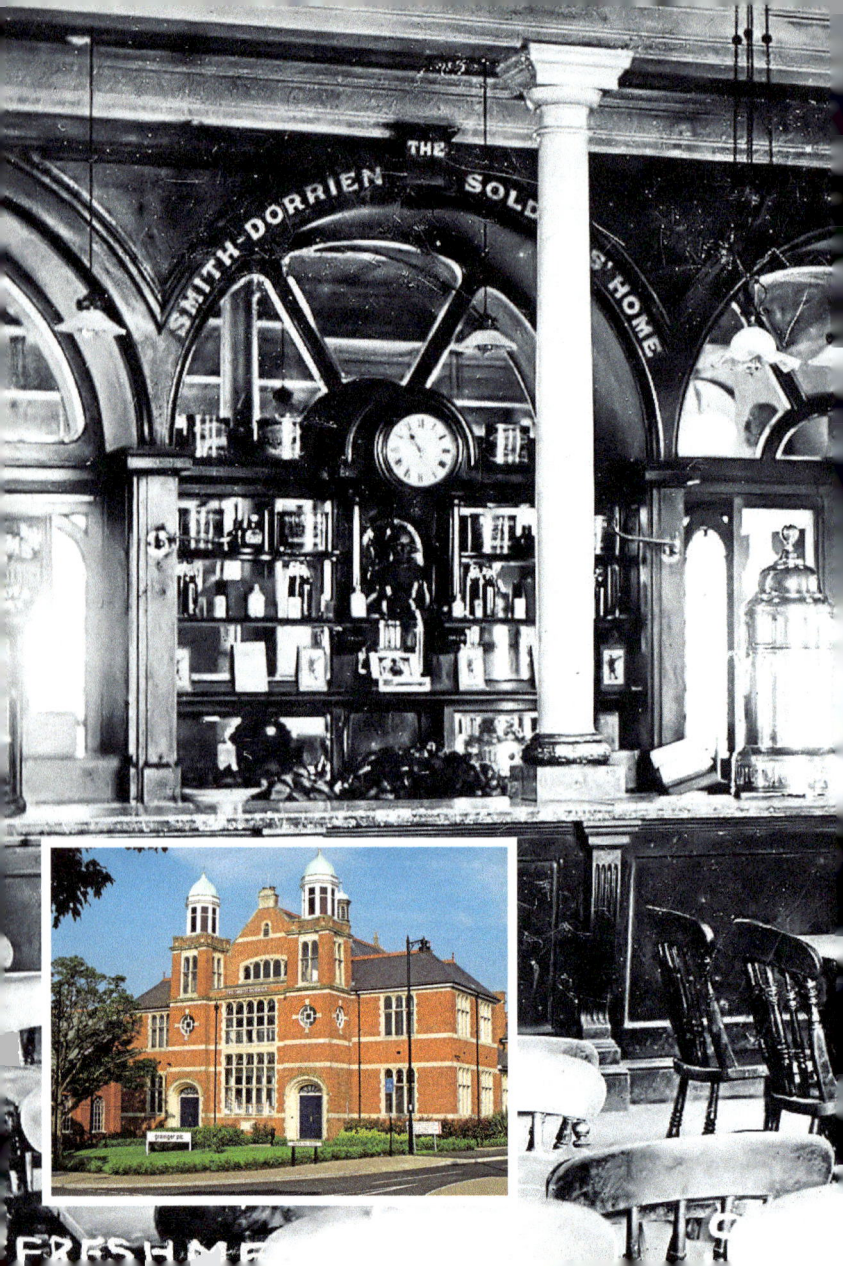

13. THE SMITH-DORRIEN SOLDIERS' HOME

For off-duty soldiers in the garrison during the late nineteenth and early twentieth centuries, the soldiers' homes provided a comfortable escape from their spartan barracks. Smith-Dorrien House at the southern end of Queen's Avenue was the Methodist soldiers' home, founded in 1908; this old photo shows the (strictly non-alcoholic) refreshment bar. The Smith-Dorrien is now offices for Grainger plc, who have recently restored it both internally and externally, and many of the original features can still be seen.

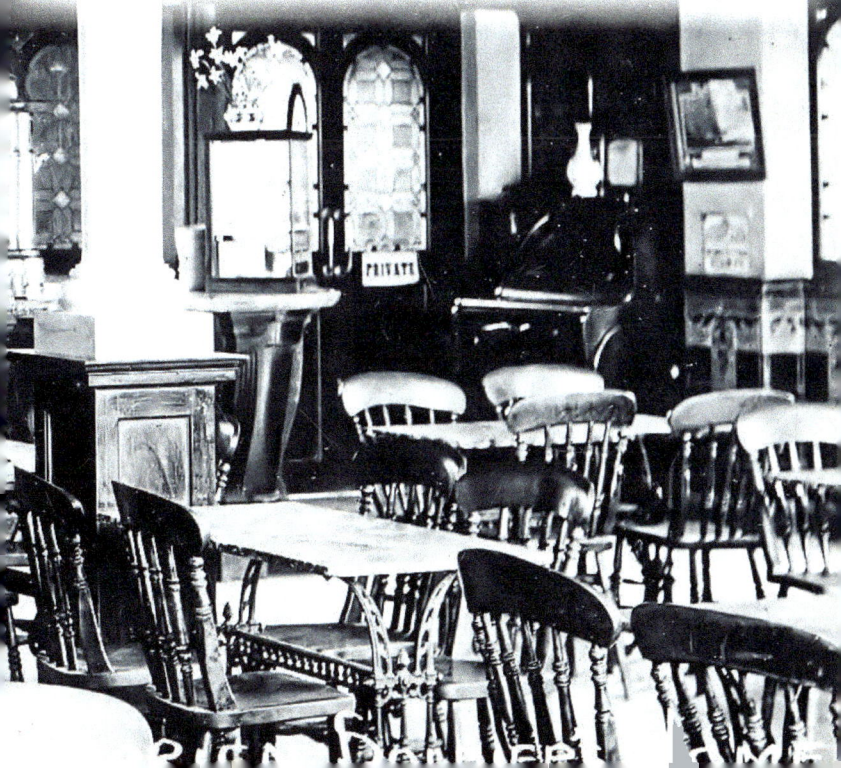

14. QUEEN'S AVENUE

The main road running through the garrison from north to south was named Queen's Avenue in 1898 by command of Queen Victoria following a particularly successful royal review of the garrison. The trees were planted in the late nineteenth century and have matured to give a most elegant avenue. The scene in the photograph from the 1930s is still easily recognisable today, with the spire of the Church of St Michael and St George a clear landmark.

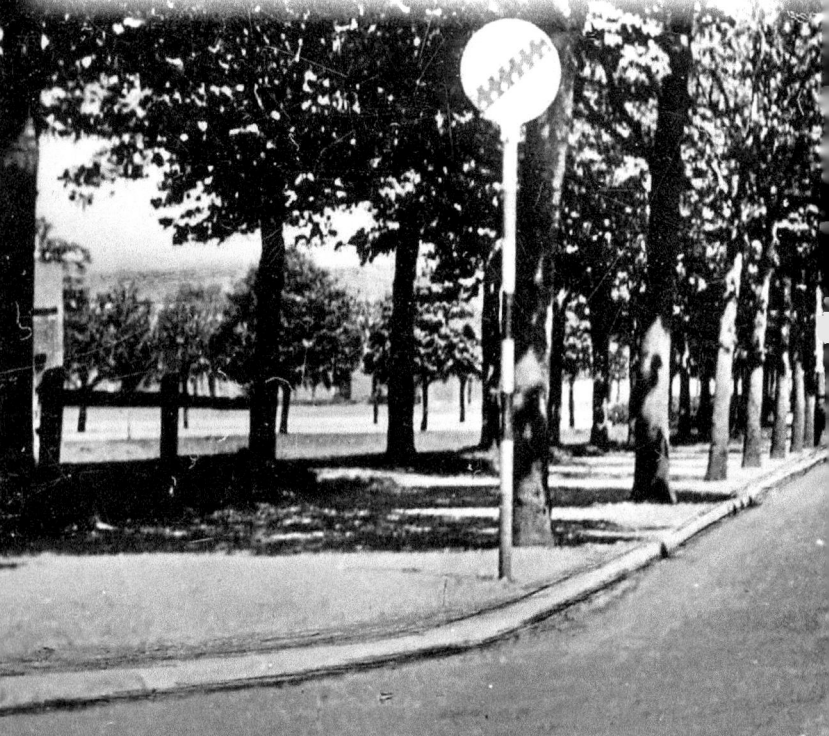

QUEENS AVENUE, ALDERSHOT.

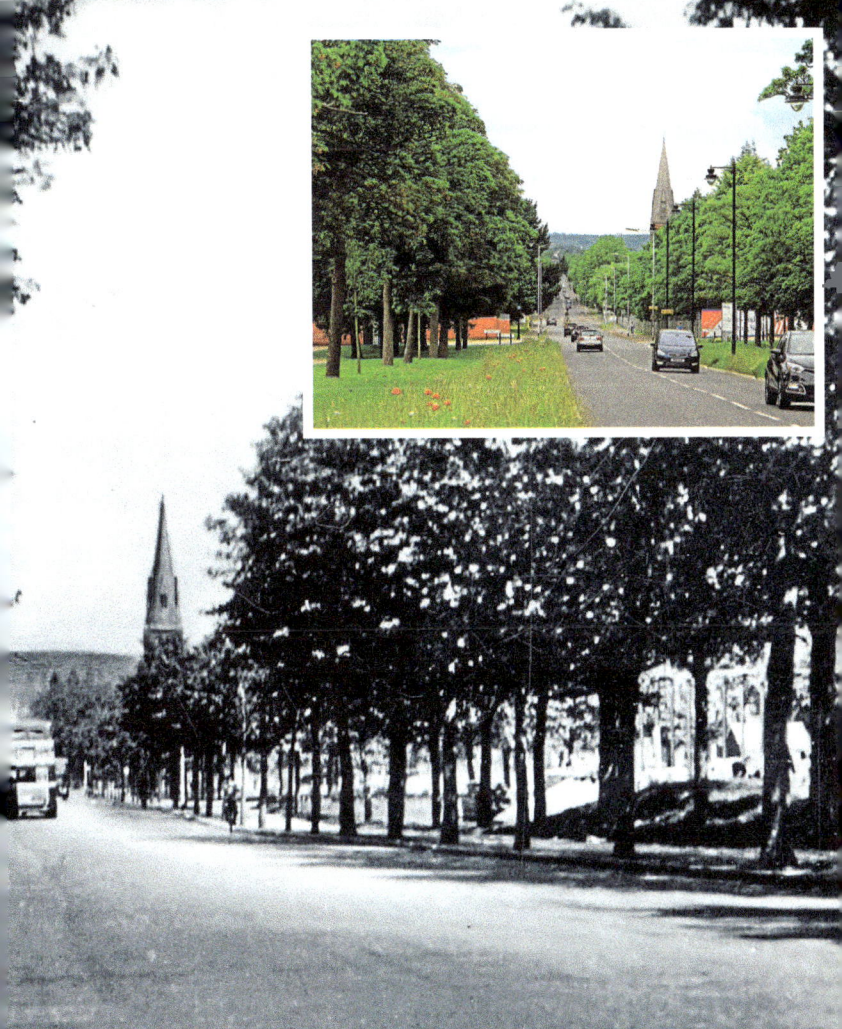

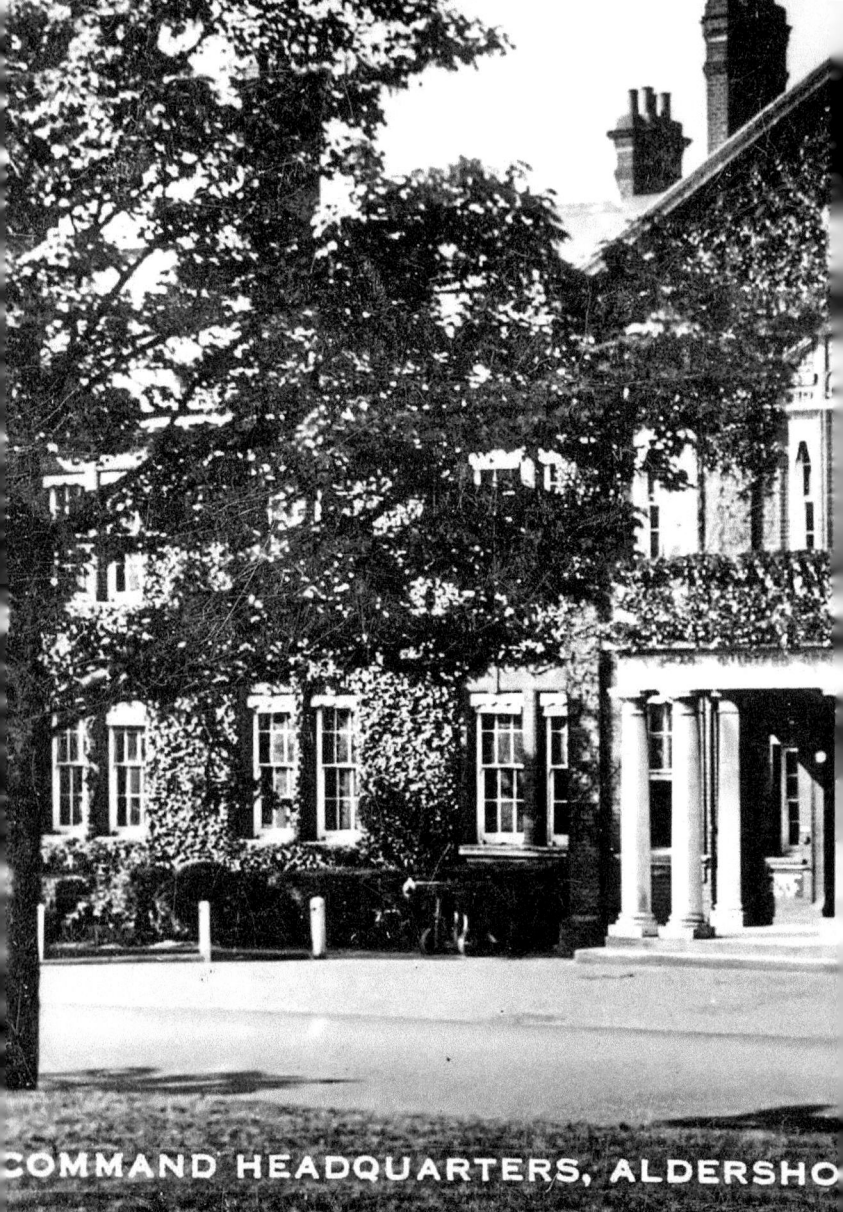

COMMAND HEADQUARTERS, ALDERSHOT

15. ALDERSHOT COMMAND HEADQUARTERS

By the end of the nineteenth century Aldershot Command had been established, taking in Aldershot garrison itself and barracks throughout the surrounding area. In 1894/95 an elegant new Command Headquarters was built. The Army vacated the building in 2014 when the HQ moved to a new building in North Camp, and the old headquarters is being converted (in 2016) for civilian use as part of the Wellesley development. The exterior of the building is largely unchanged today.

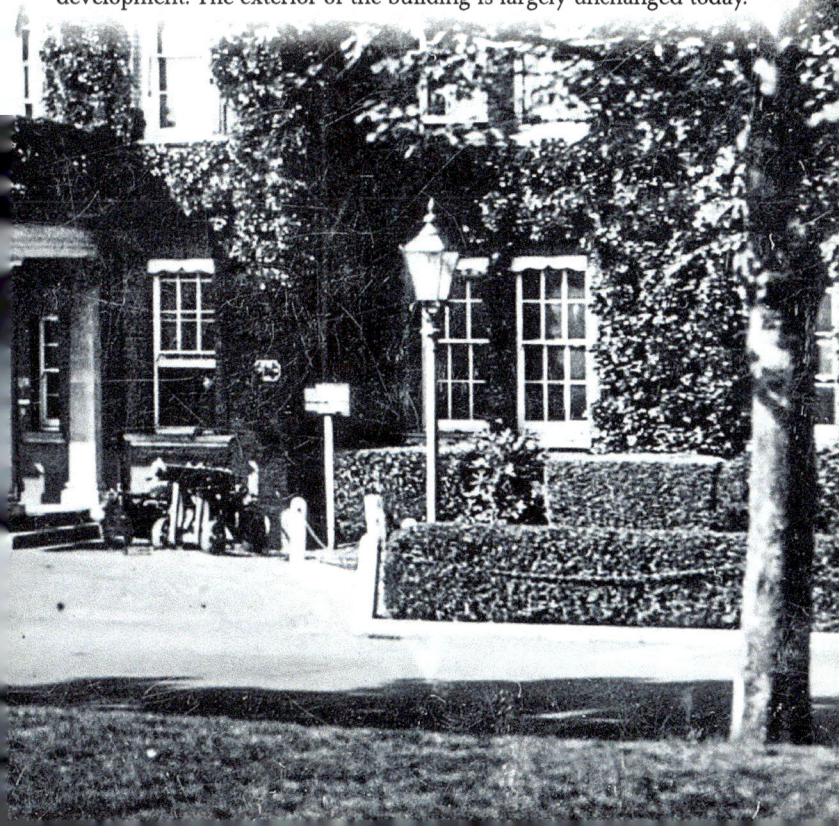

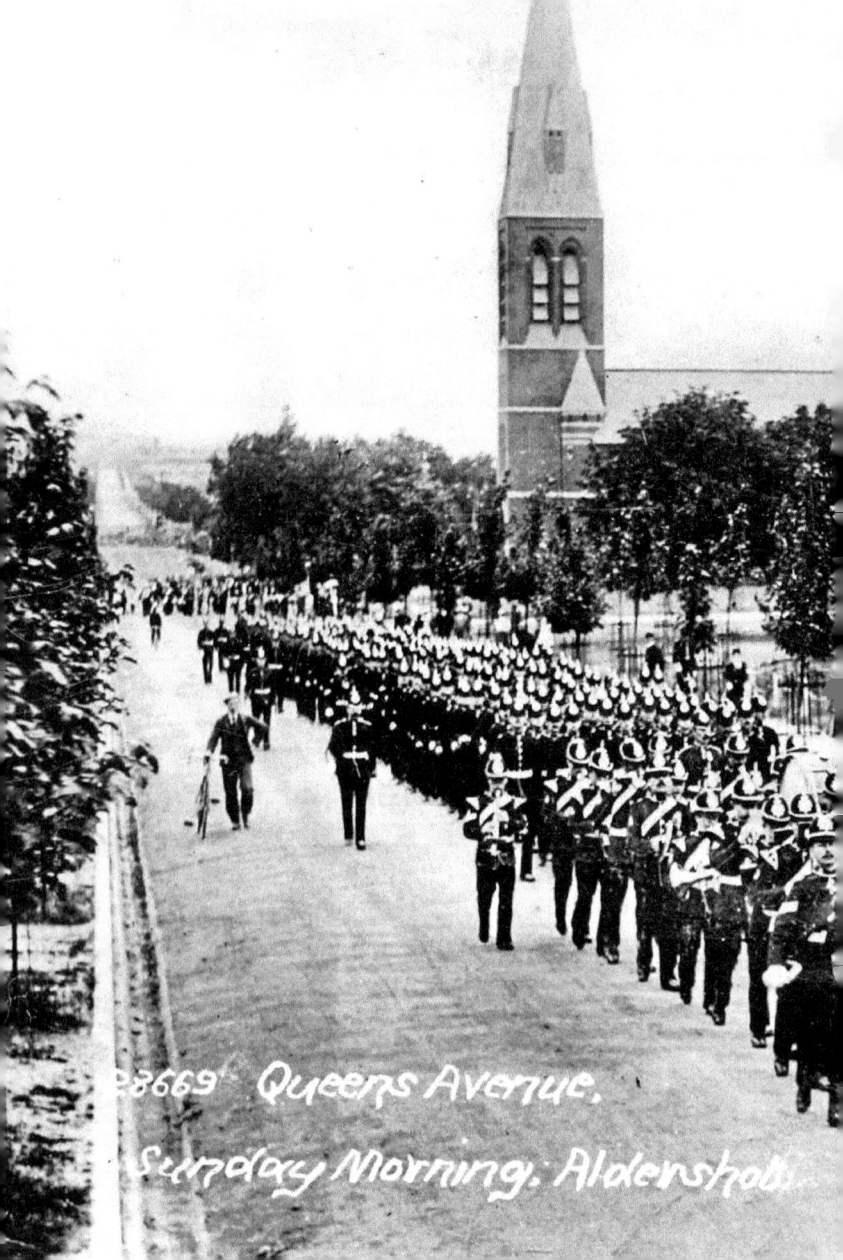

16. CHURCH OF ST MICHAEL AND ST GEORGE

When the garrison was rebuilt in the 1890s another church was built to cope with the growing numbers of soldiers. Queen Victoria laid the foundation stone for the Church of St George in 1892, and this photograph shows a church parade from 1912. Since 1973 the church has been the Roman Catholic garrison church and named St Michael and St George. It is also the cathedral church of the Roman Catholic Bishop of the Forces.

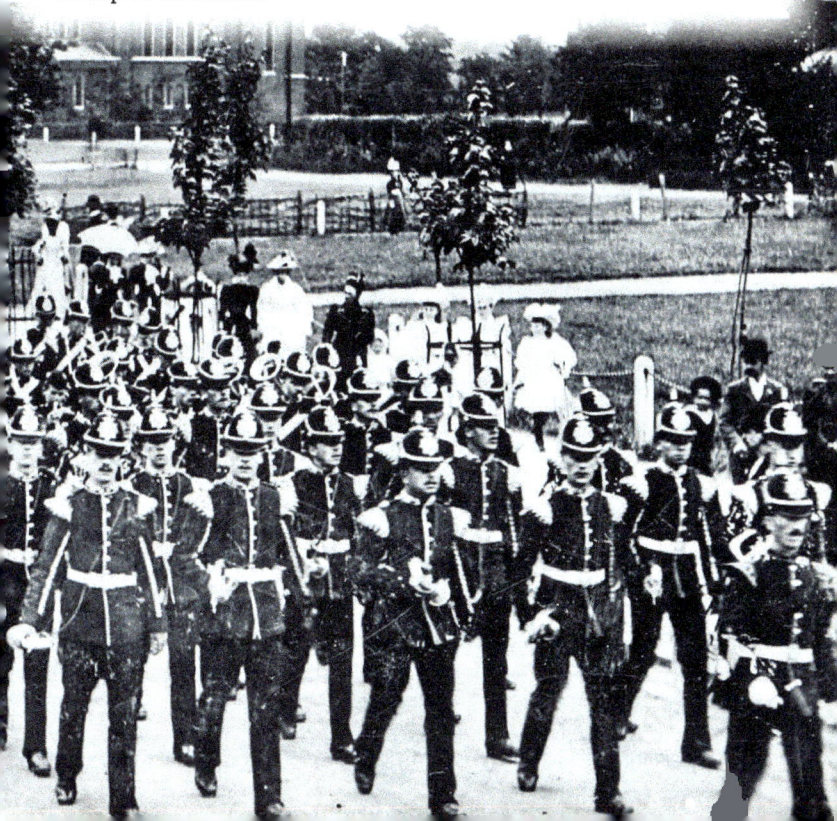

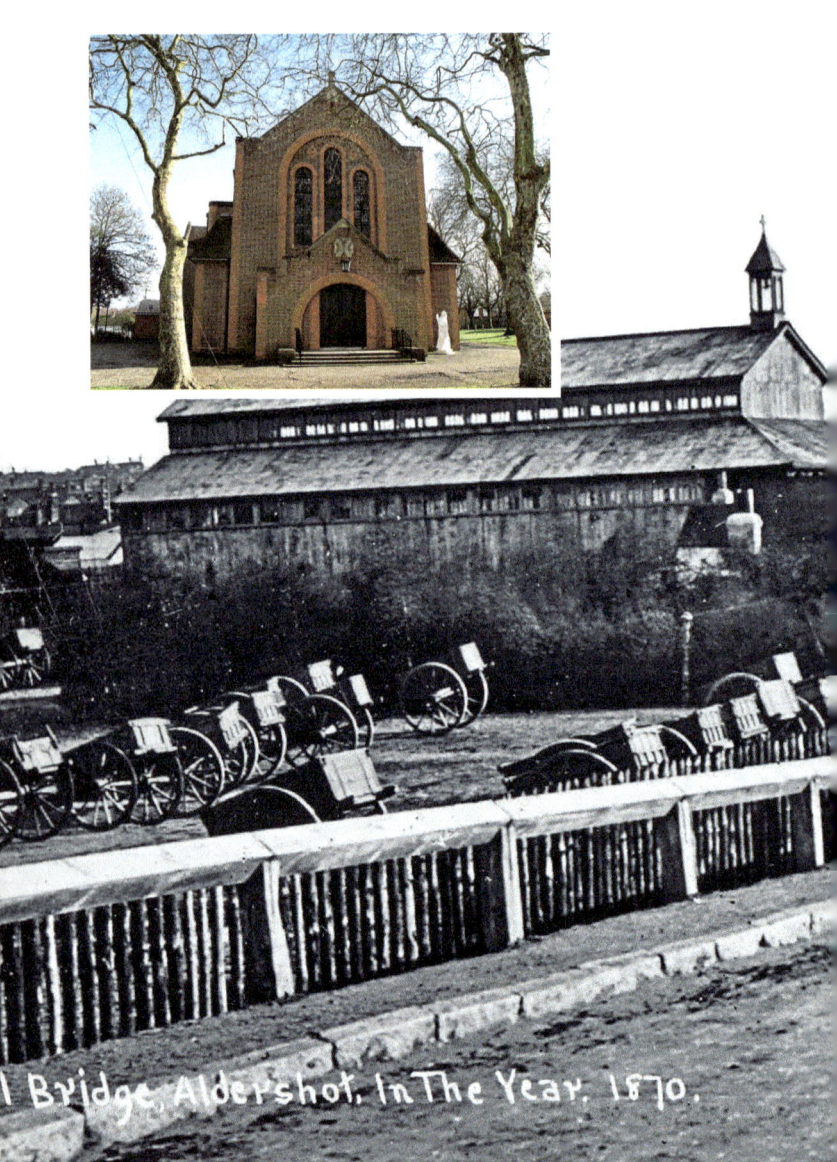

17. THE IRON CHURCH

The photograph from 1870 is taken from the old Wooden Bridge over the Basingstoke Canal (the site of the current Iron Bridge) and looks over to the Iron Church, so named because its walls were hung on an iron framework, with iron pillars and a tin roof. This was the first garrison church, originally sited near Thorn Hill and moved to this location in 1866. It was dismantled in 1926 and St Andrew's Church, the Garrison Church of Scotland, was built on the site.

The tour continues into North Camp. If you want to miss out this part, go back to the traffic lights, turn right on Alison's Road, then go left on Farnborough Road until you are opposite Potter's International Hotel, then continue from stop No. 21.

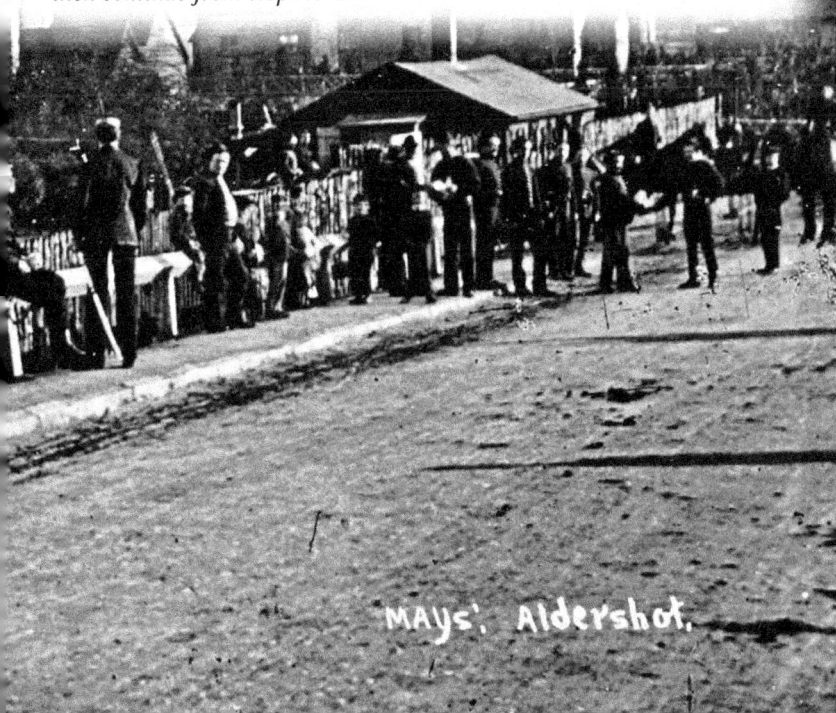

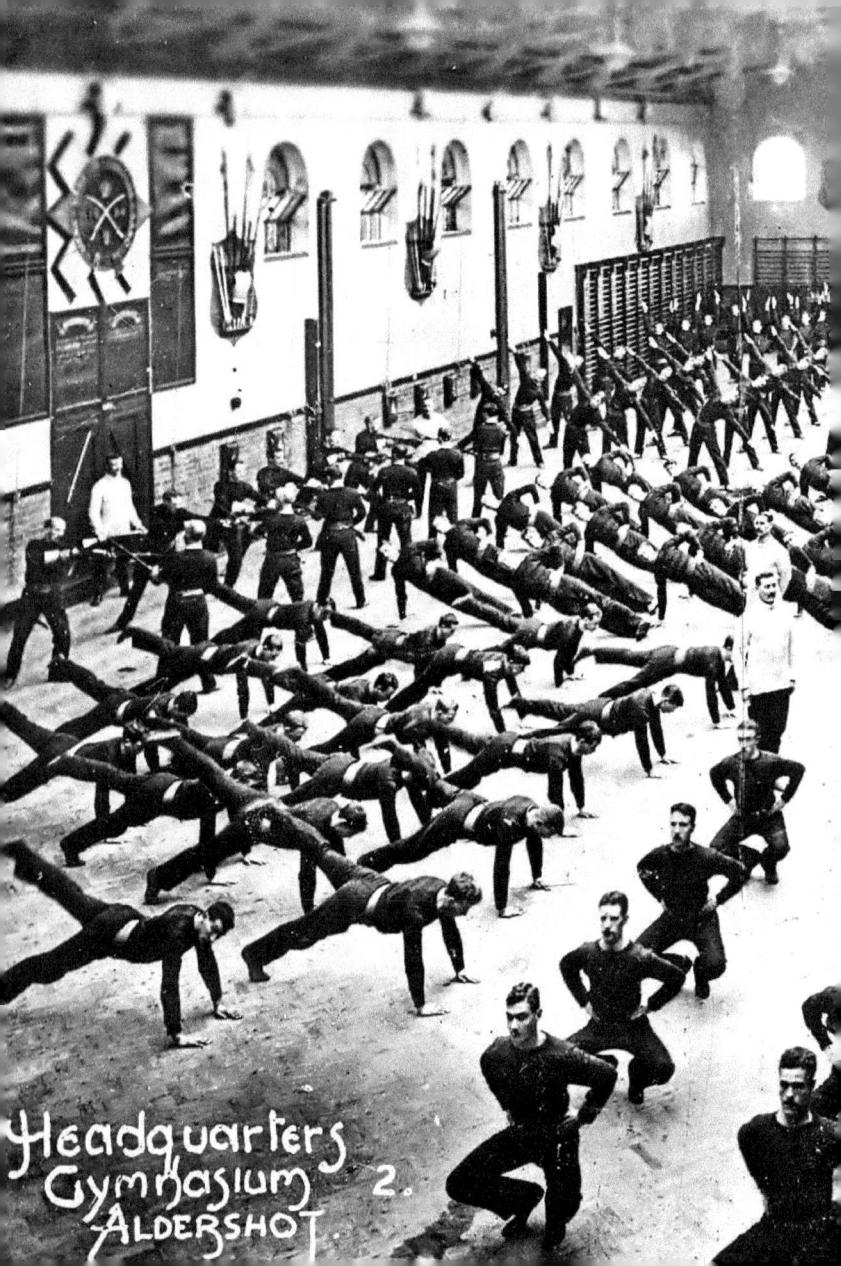

18. THE FOX GYMNASIUM

The first army gymnasium was built in 1860, but in 1894 a new and much larger gymnasium was built at the instigation of Col Malcolm Fox, Inspector of Gymnasia from 1890 to 1897. This is within the Army School of Physical Training and is still in use today. This old photograph from 1918 shows the interior of the gym with the NCOs who were passing out as PT instructors, carefully posed to show off their skills.

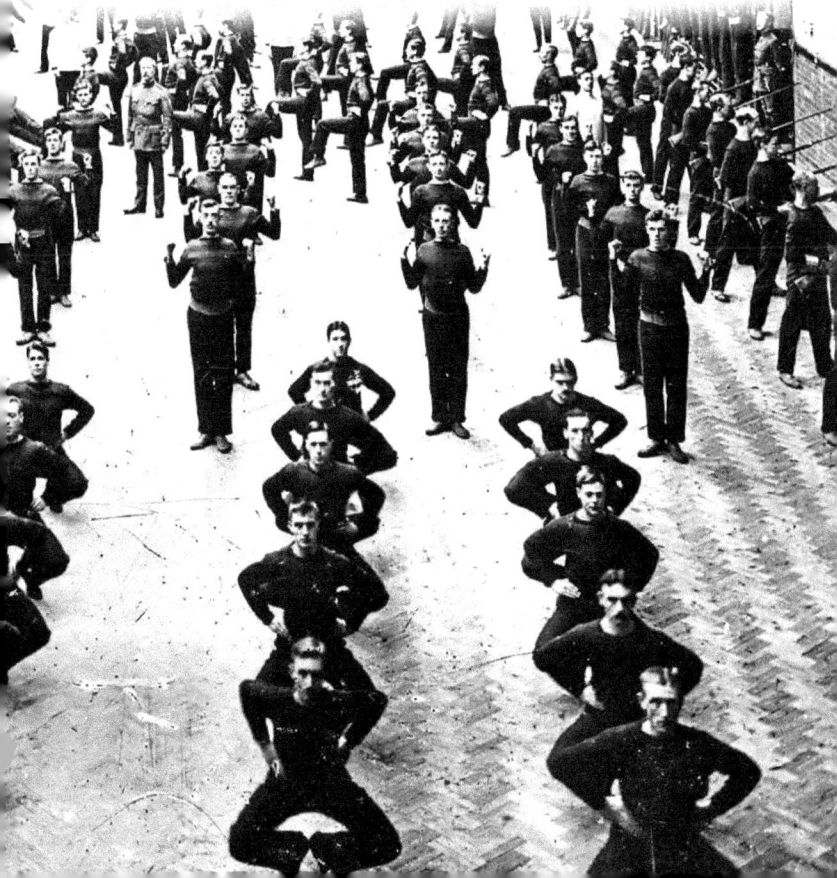

19. OUDENARDE BARRACKS

The camp was originally just wooden huts, but in the 1890s these were replaced in North Camp with single-storey barrack blocks, one per company (approximately thirty men). Oudenarde Barracks was one of a series of infantry barracks that made up Marlborough Lines. This historic photo shows the Black Watch parading in 1913, with soldiers' barracks on the right and the officers' mess behind. Only two of the Victorian barracks blocks remain and are now used for the excellent Aldershot Military Museum.

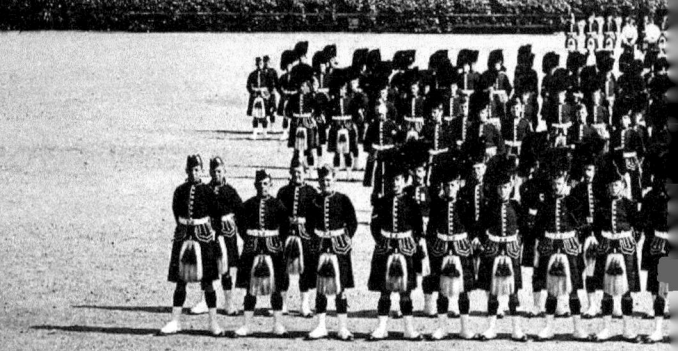

CHURCH. PARADE. BLACK. WATCH

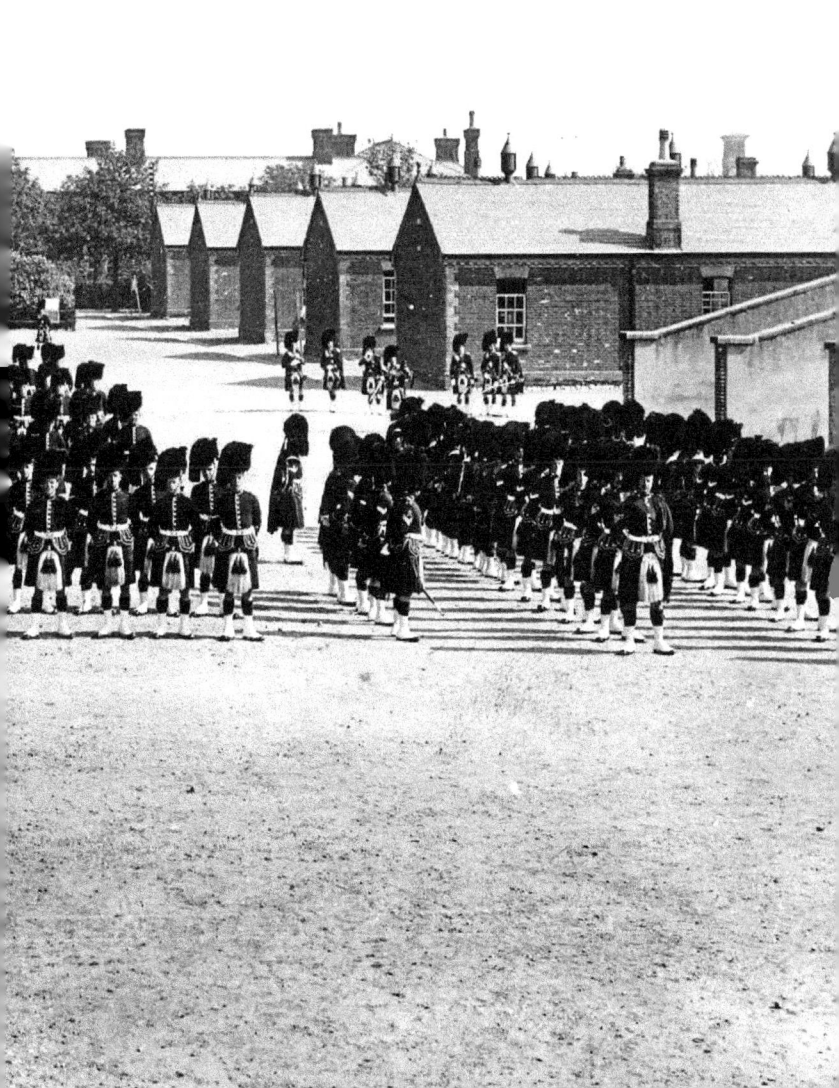

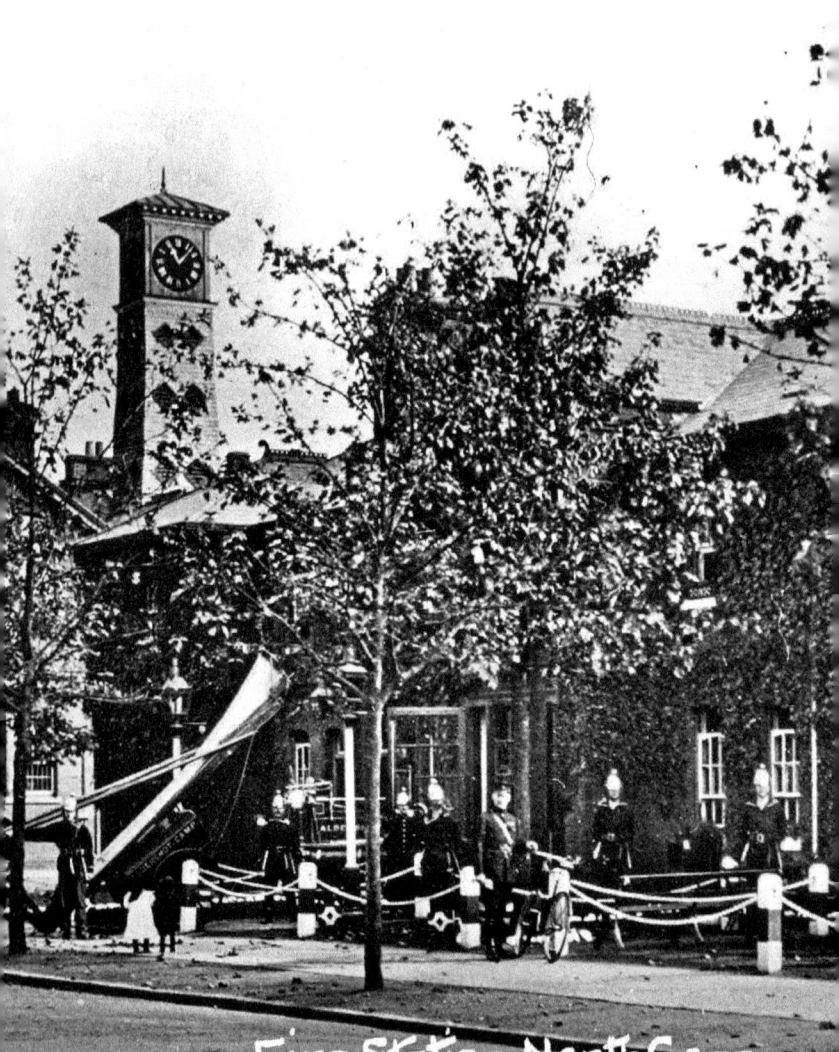

20. CLOCKTOWER SCHOOL AND FIRE STATION

There were fire stations in both North and South Camps, each with a fully equipped fire brigade. In the photo from 1910 the men of the North Camp brigade pose outside the station in their polished brass helmets. Behind is the clock tower of the North Camp infants' school. This building still stands and is used for a playgroup, but the fire station is no more and its site is just open space.

Continue up Queen's Avenue to the roundabout, turn left onto Lynchford Road, and then left onto Farnborough Road. Continue south until you are opposite Potter's International Hotel.

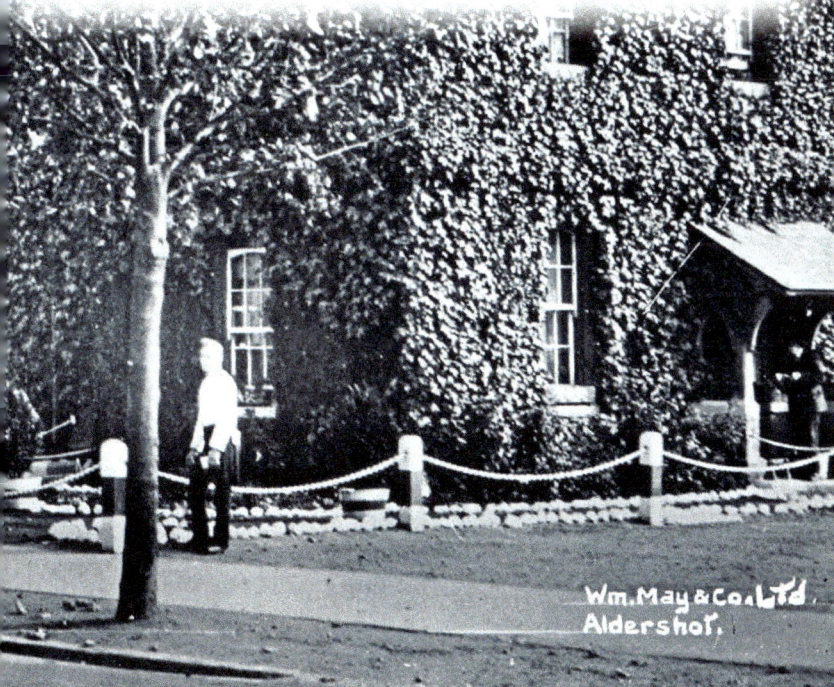

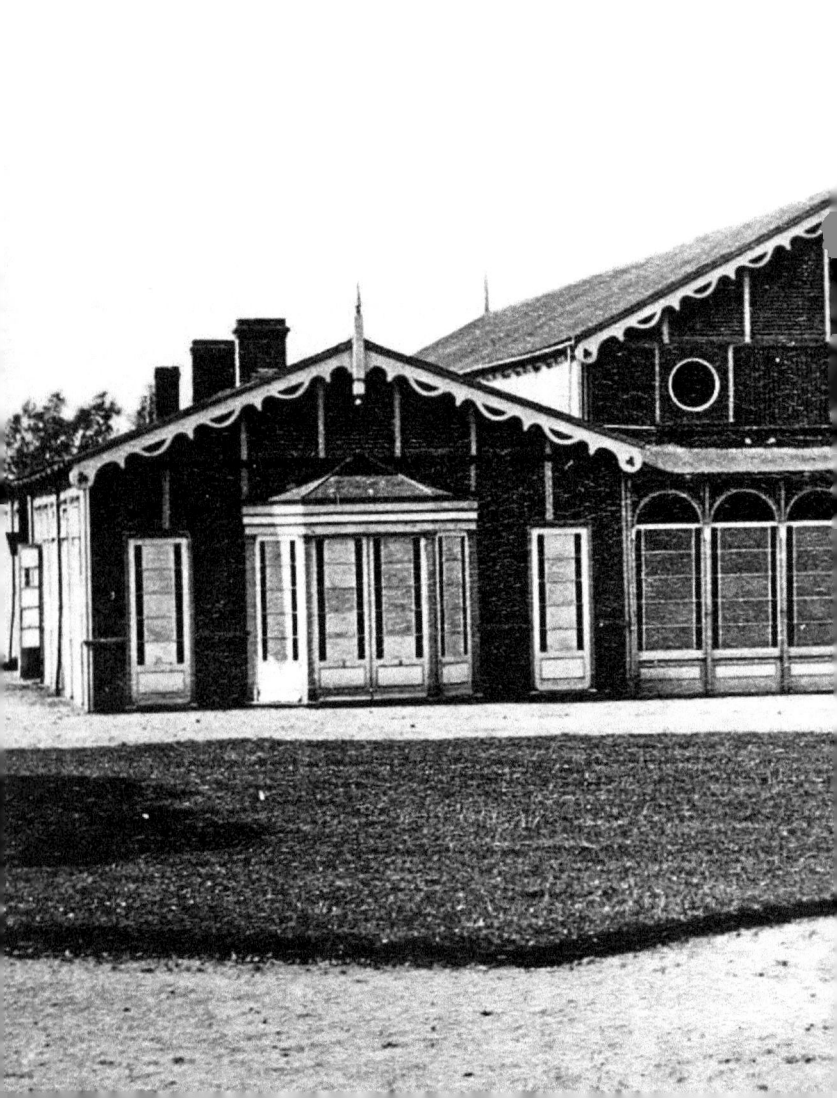

21. THE OFFICERS' CLUB

The Aldershot Officers' Club was established in 1859 as somewhere for the army officers to take their meals and spend time off duty, before the establishment of proper officers' messes. It was very popular and expanded to include a ballroom, games rooms, a reading room, and many sporting facilities. In the late twentieth century declining membership resulted in its redevelopment as Potters International Hotel, which at the back retains part of the old building for the officers' club.

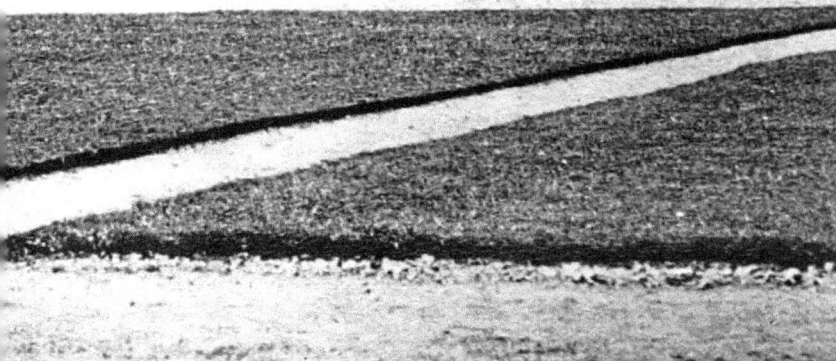

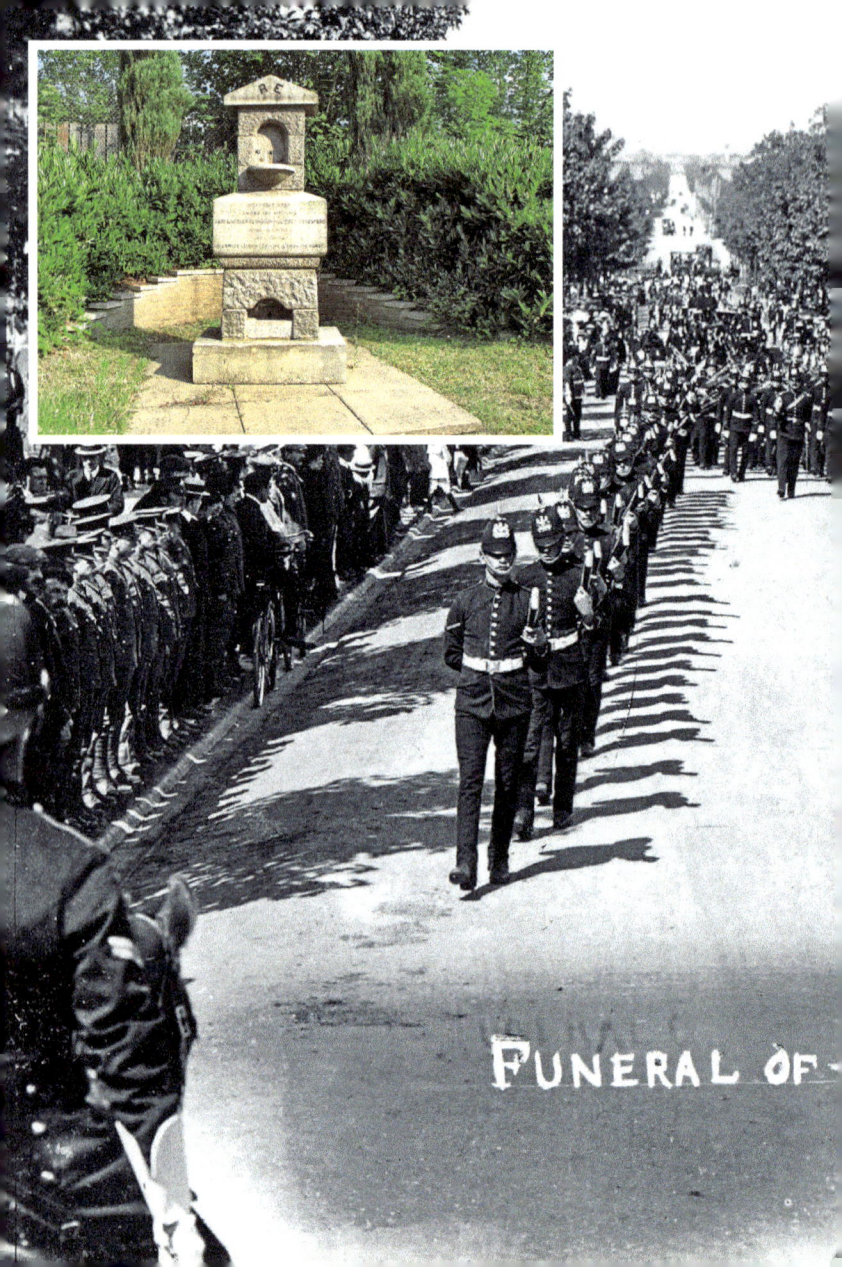

FUNERAL OF

22. BERESFORD MEMORIAL

This horses' drinking fountain was erected on the Farnborough Road in 1910 to mark the place where Capt. Charles Beresford of the Royal Engineers lost his life in a brave attempt to stop a runaway horse that was endangering passers-by. In recognition of his selfless act, Beresford was honoured by a huge military funeral and the long procession marched up Queen's Avenue en route to the Military Cemetery.

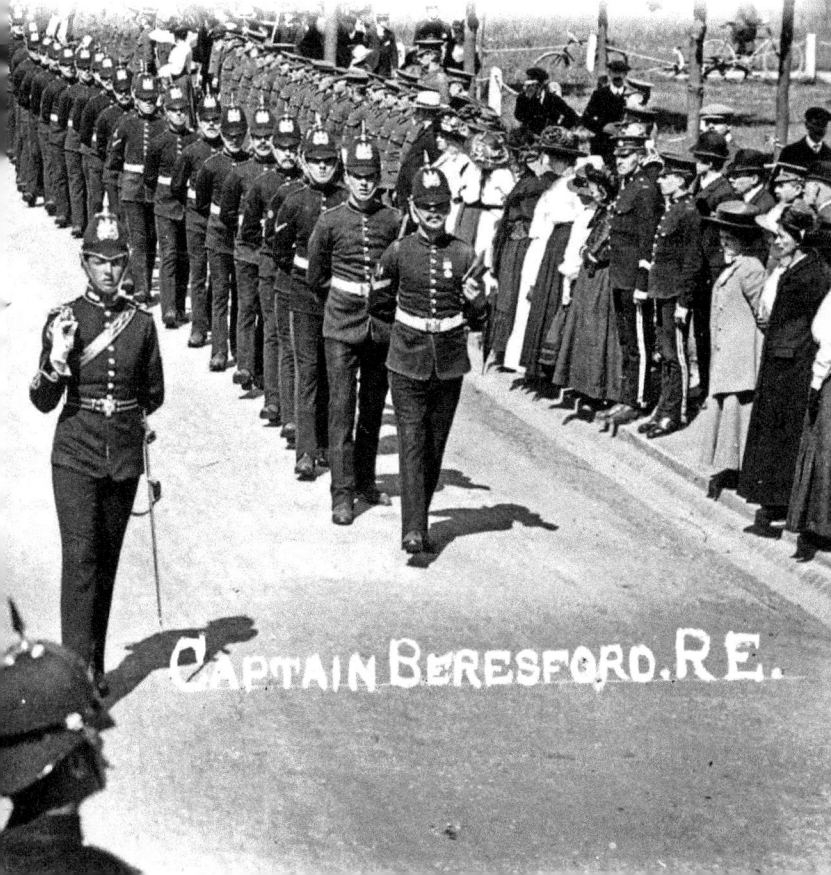

23. THE PRINCE CONSORT'S LIBRARY

Opened in 1860, this was founded and funded by the Prince Consort as a military library for the Army in Aldershot. In this photograph from the 1870s, the first librarian, Sgt Charles Gilmore, stands on the left with his orderly on the right. An extension, to the left of the building in this picture, was built in 1911. The library is only open to serving army personnel, but the building can be seen from Knollys Road.

Continue south on Farnborough Road and cross at the light-controlled crossing, then bear right on the road past the church.

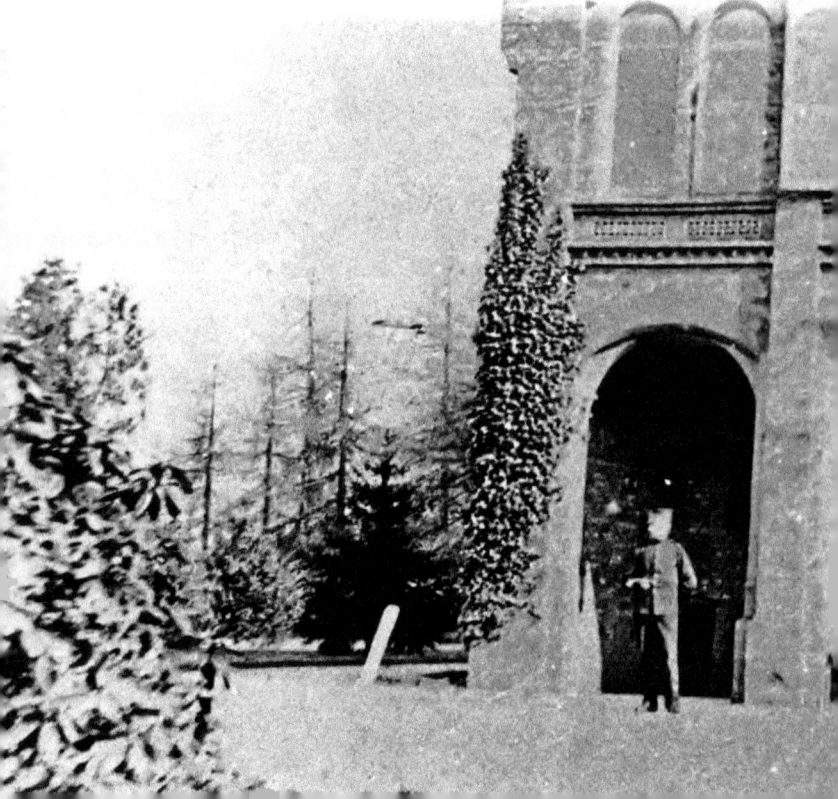

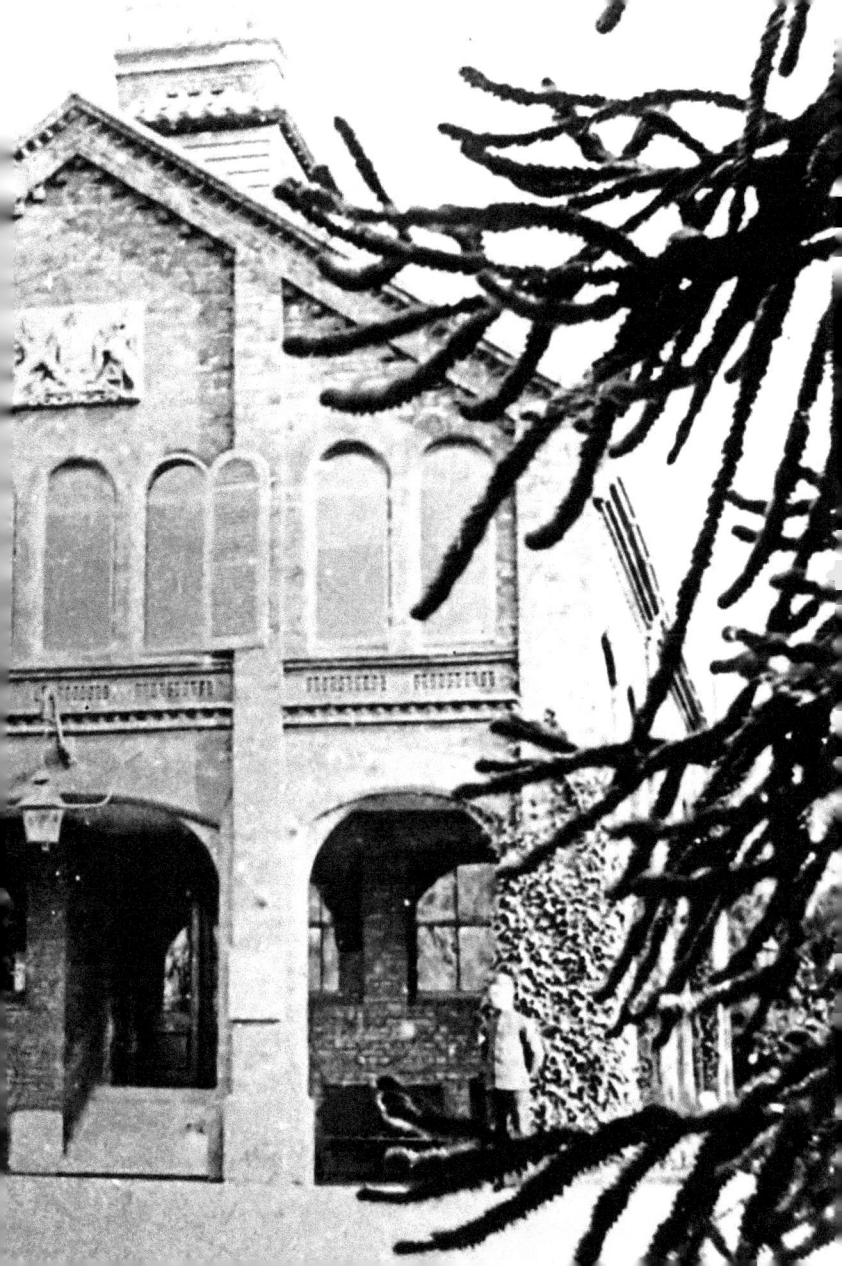

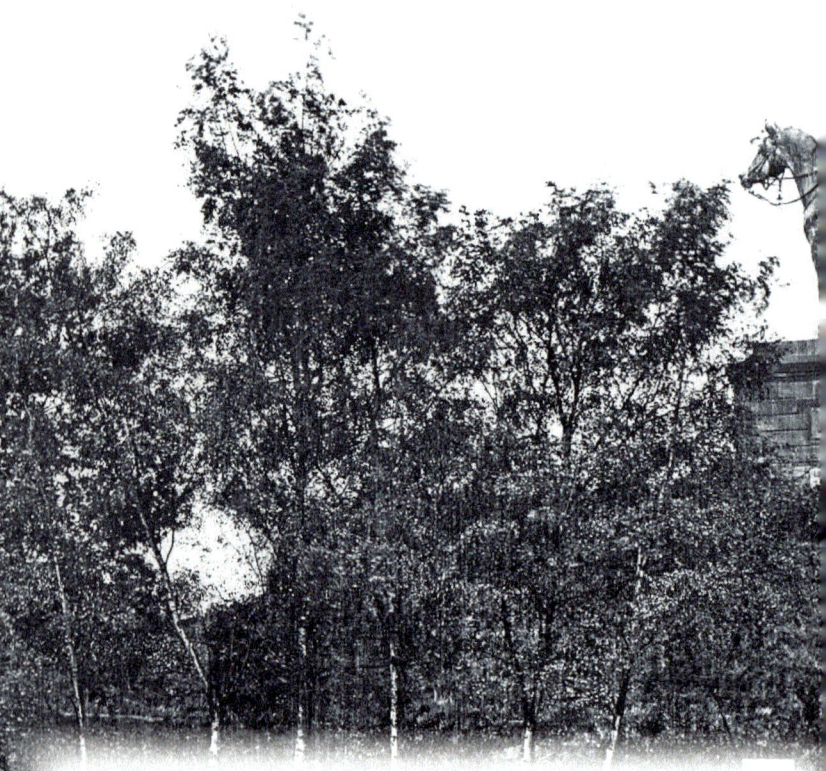

24. THE WELLINGTON STATUE

Still the largest equestrian statue in the country at 28 feet high, the great Wellington Statue by Matthew Cotes Wyatt originally stood on the arch at Hyde Park Corner in London. It was re-erected in Aldershot in 1885 on Round Hill, adjacent to the Royal Garrison Church, and became a symbol of Aldershot's military heritage. This historic photograph shows the statue in around 1920. In the early twenty-first century the statue was cleaned and restored and the surrounding landscape much improved.

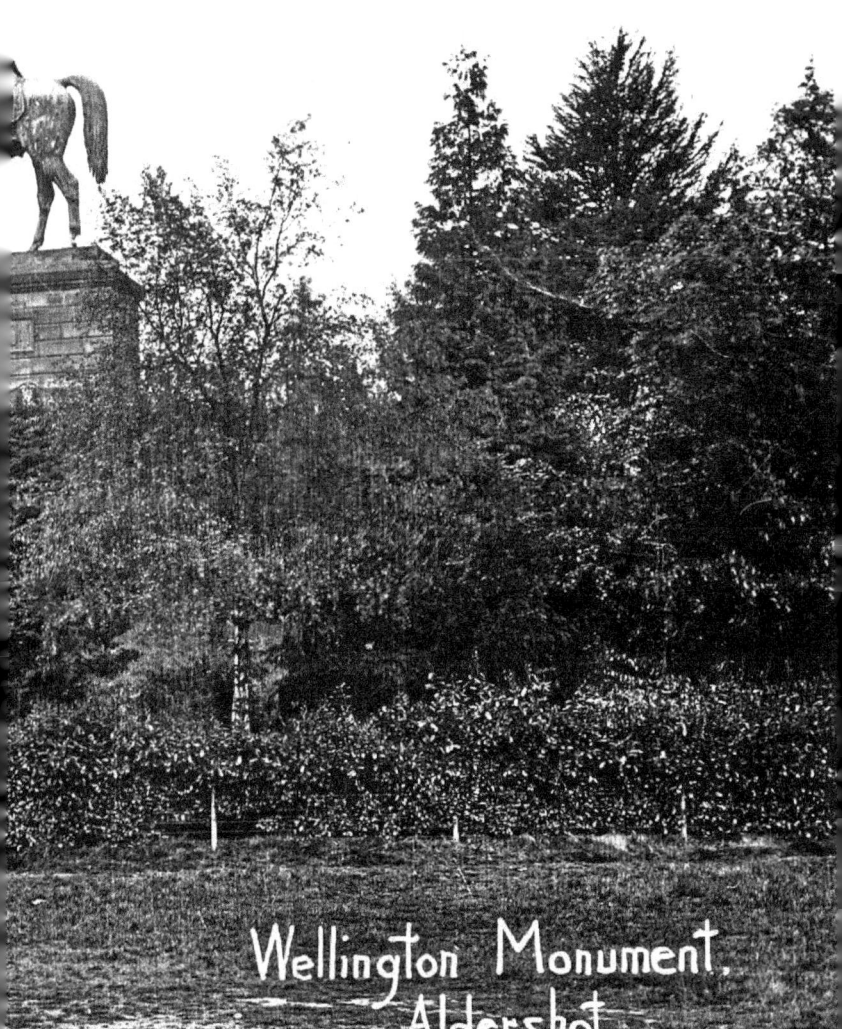

Wellington Monument, Aldershot.
A.891.

25. ROYAL GARRISON CHURCH OF ALL SAINTS

A suitable garrison church was needed for the camp, so the Church of All Saints was built west of the Farnborough Road and dedicated on 29 July 1863. The church was granted the title 'Royal' by George V in 1923, in recognition of its Diamond Jubilee. The early photo, c. 1912, shows crowds watching one of the regular Sunday church parades. The building itself is little changed, but church parades are now rare events.

Continue south on Farnborough Road, following the path that crosses Wellesley Road.

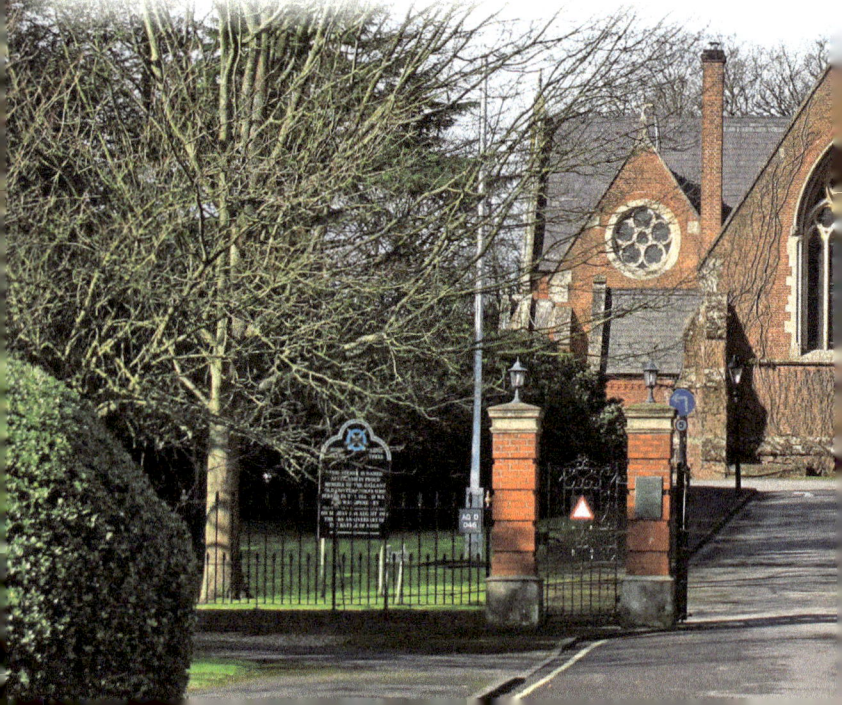

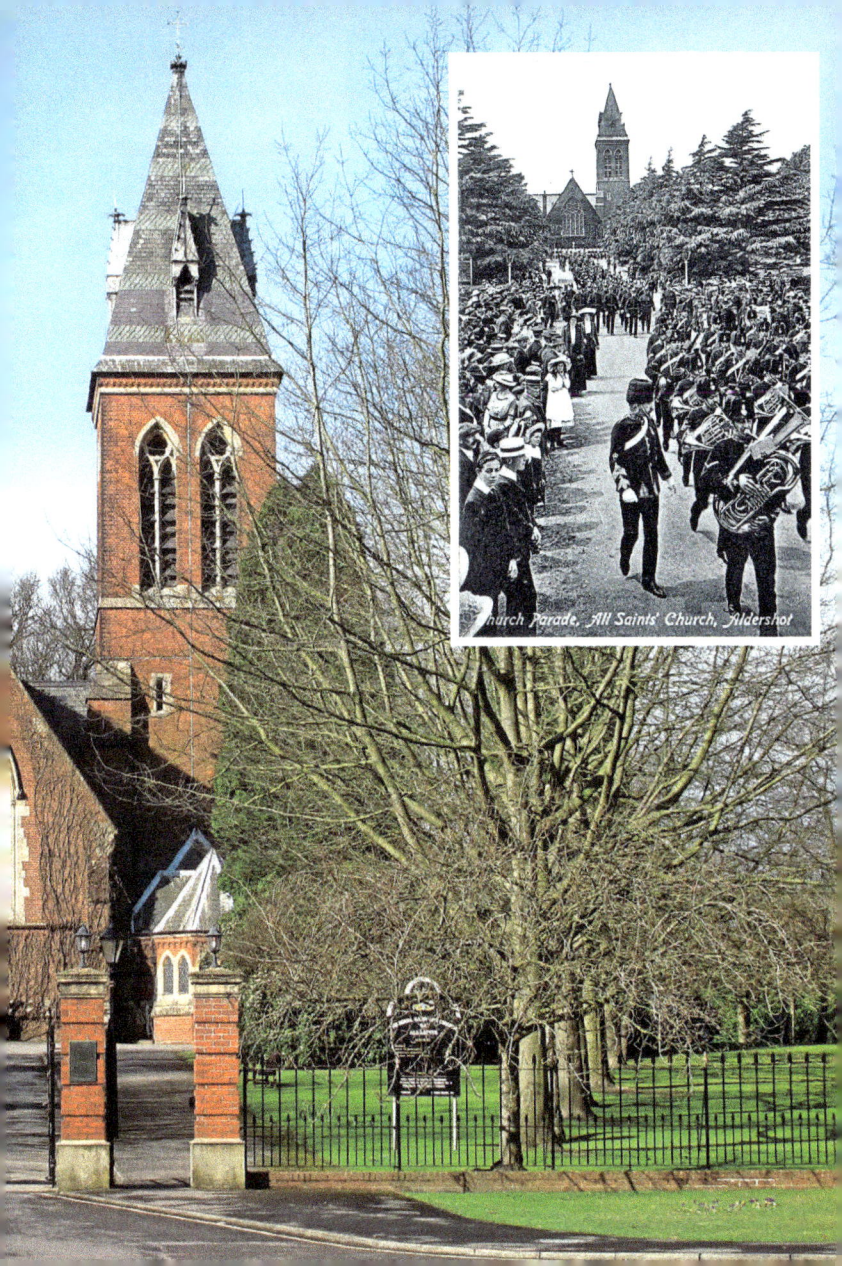

Church Parade, All Saints' Church, Aldershot

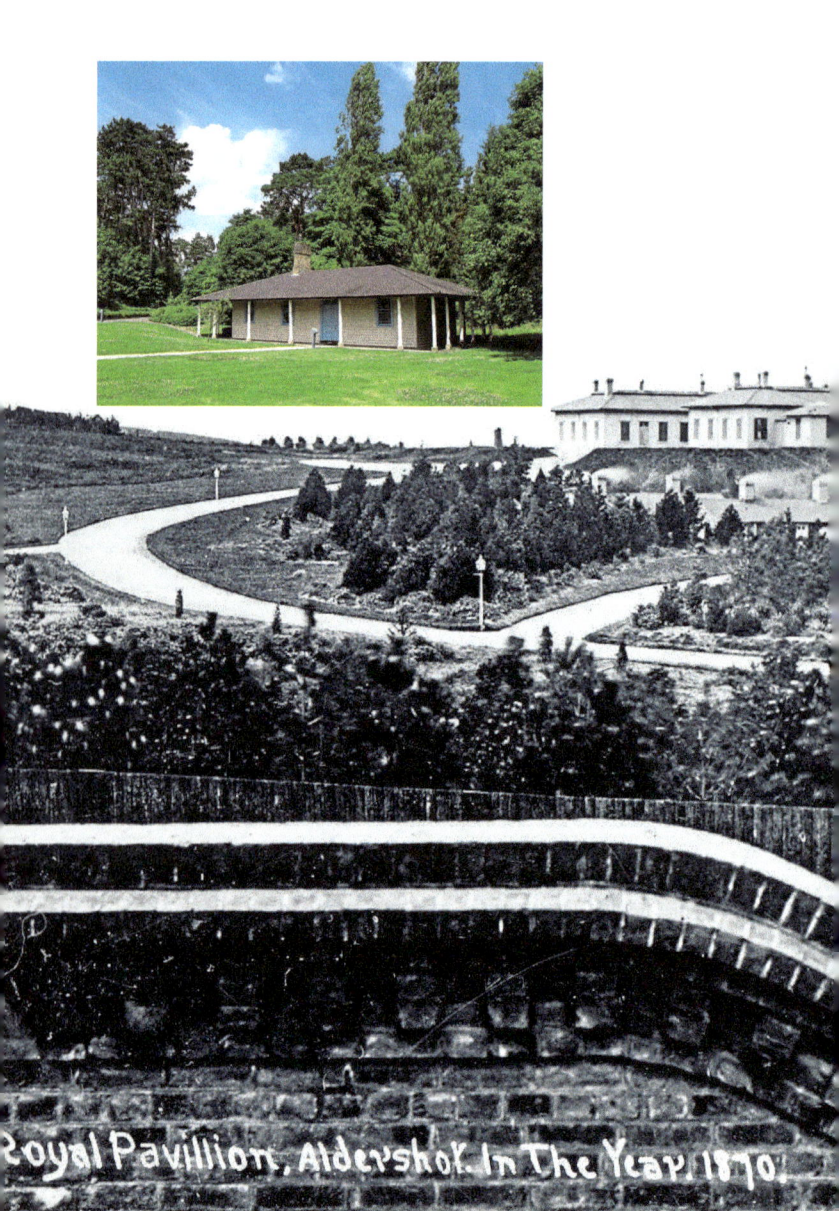

26. THE ROYAL PAVILION

Seen from the South Cavalry Barracks in this picture from 1870, the Royal Pavilion was a wooden bungalow built in 1856 for the royal family to use when visiting Aldershot. It was demolished in 1963 and the QARANC Training Centre built on the site, which in turn has been replaced by the Computer Sciences Corporation offices. All that is left of the original Pavilion is the guardroom, the only surviving wooden building from the early camp.

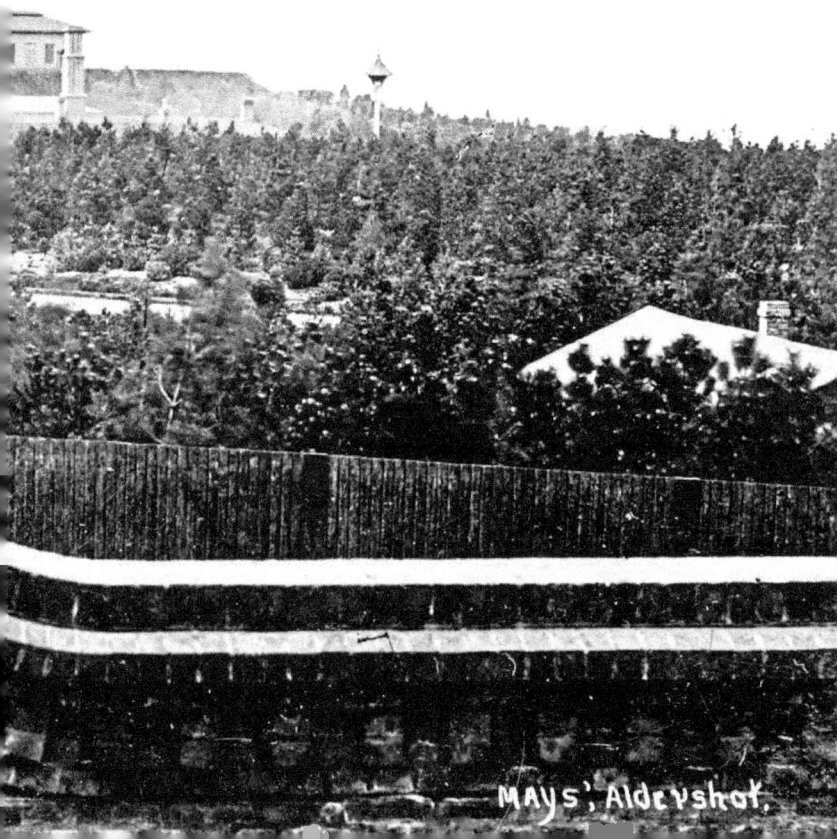

27. SOUTH CAVALRY BARRACKS GATES

This remarkable early photograph shows the construction of the gates to the South Cavalry Barracks (later named Beaumont Barracks) in 1856. These were some of the first permanent barracks to be built in Aldershot. Although the barracks are gone, the gates on the Farnborough Road still stand, along with the guardrooms behind which are used by the Beaumont Park playgroup.

Retrace your steps to the light-controlled crossing by the Royal Garrison Church. Cross over Farnborough Road and follow the path on the right to the old barracks gates by the roundabout.

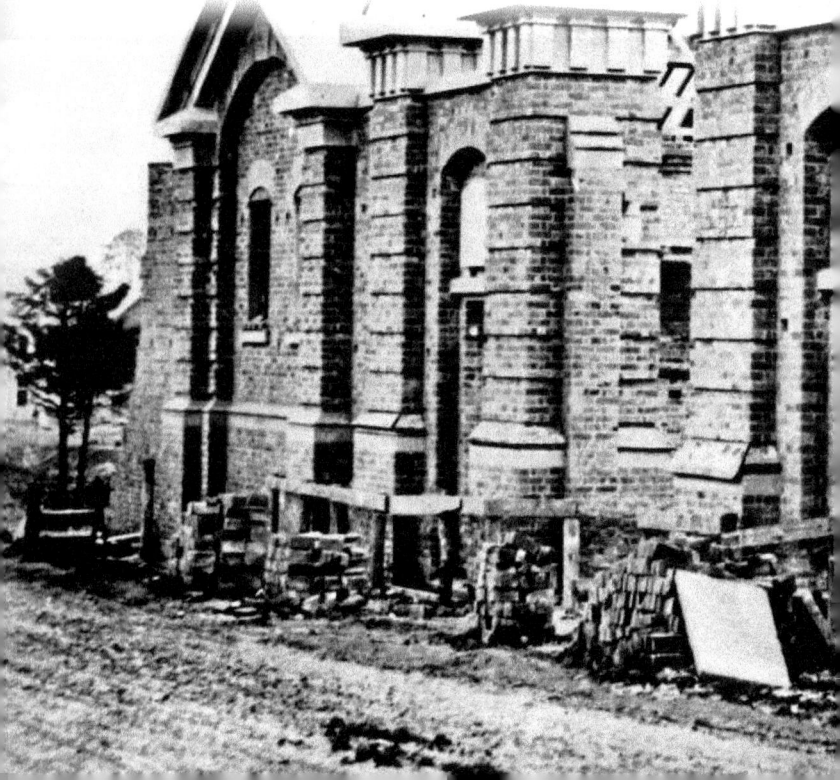

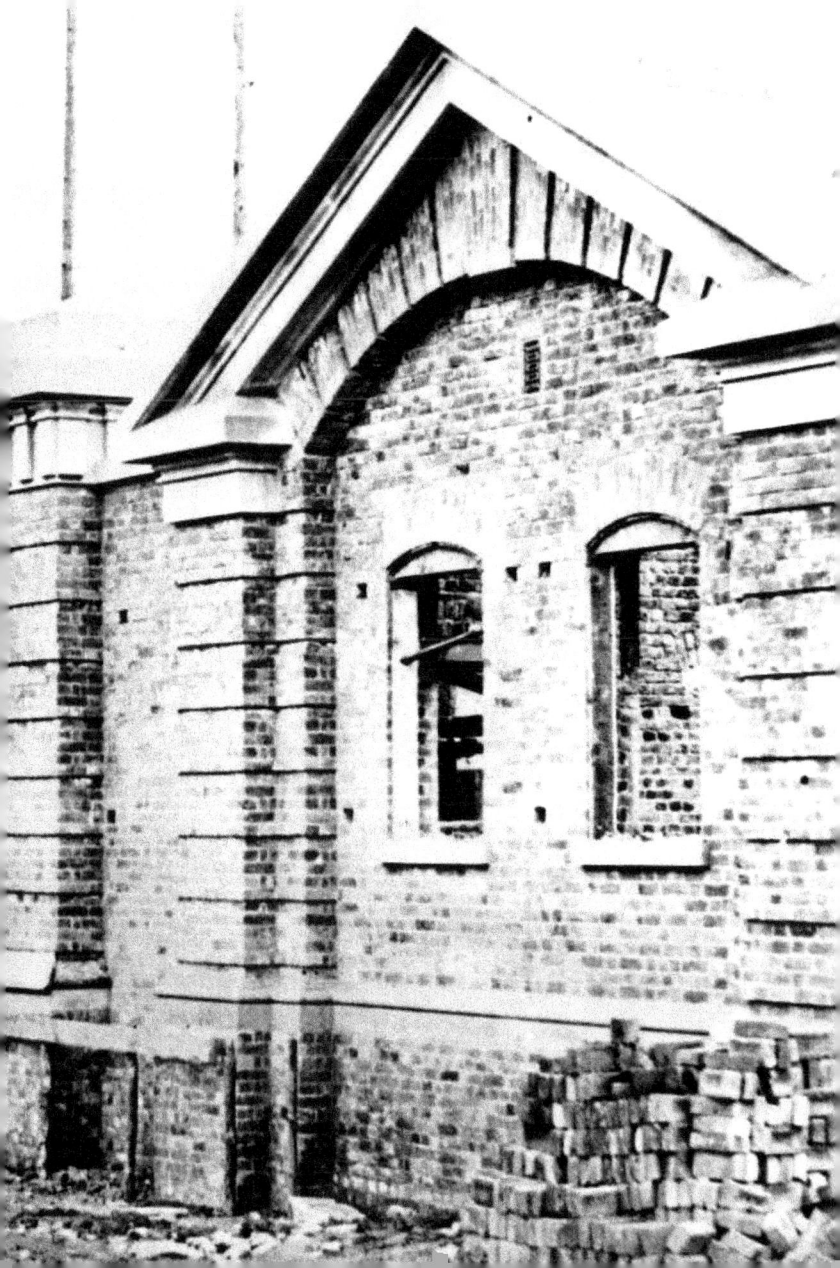

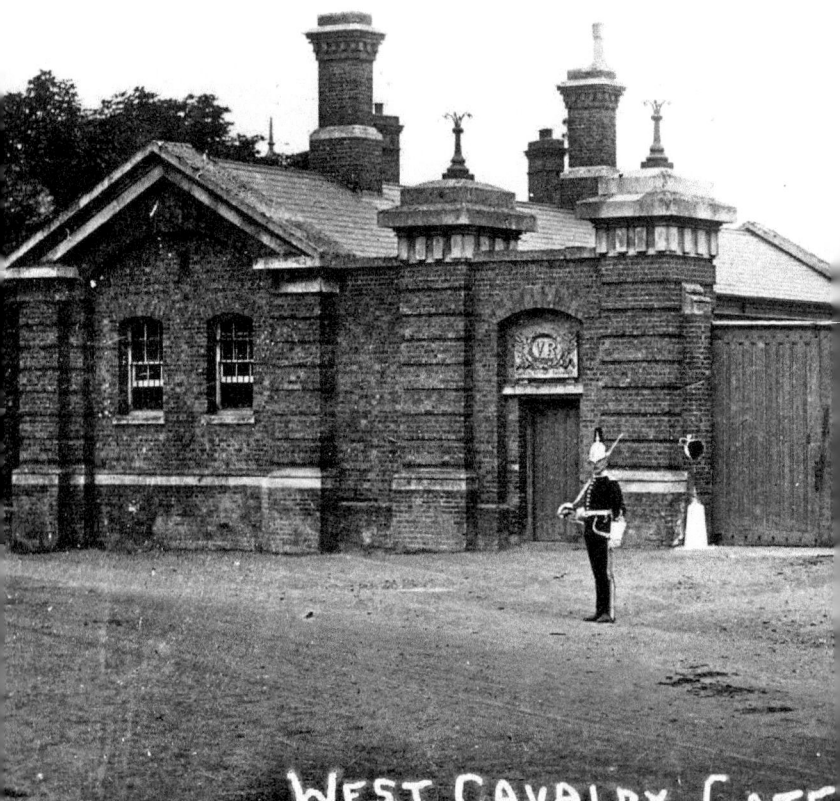
West Cavalry Gate

28. WEST CAVALRY BARRACKS GATES

Also built between 1856 and 1859, the West Cavalry Barracks (named Willems Barracks from 1909) also had its entrance onto the Farnborough Road. The Victorian barracks were demolished in the 1960s, and nothing remains except for the gates on the roundabout at the Farnborough Road junction with Wellington Avenue. Behind the gates are the Willems Park pub and Travelodge hotel.

Follow the path between the hotel and pub, walk around Tesco's superstore and through the car park to Willems Avenue. Cross over and walk up Fermor Drive to Badajos Road.

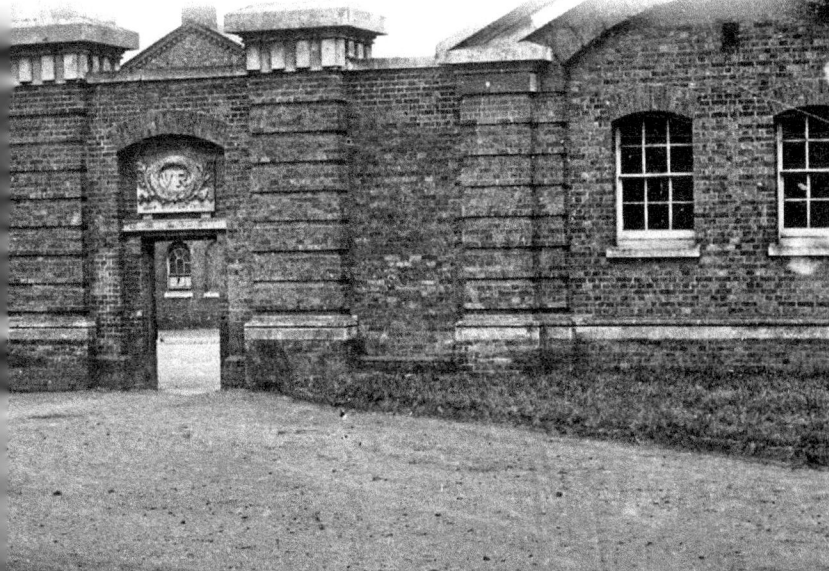

29. THE FIRST INFANTRY BARRACKS

Built at the same time as the cavalry barracks were three infantry barracks: East, Centre and West blocks, until renamed Badajos, Salamanca and Talavera in 1898. This old photograph from 1860 is an early view of the newly completed barracks. All were demolished after the Second World War, and on the site today are the modern army married quarters of Salamanca Park.

Go east along Badajos Road to Hospital Hill.

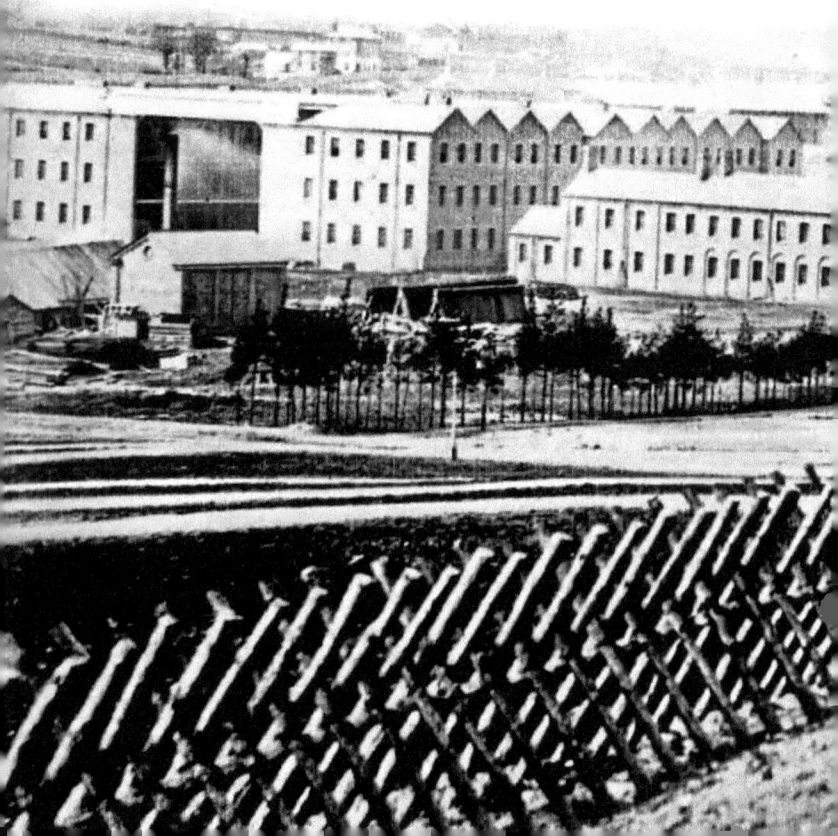

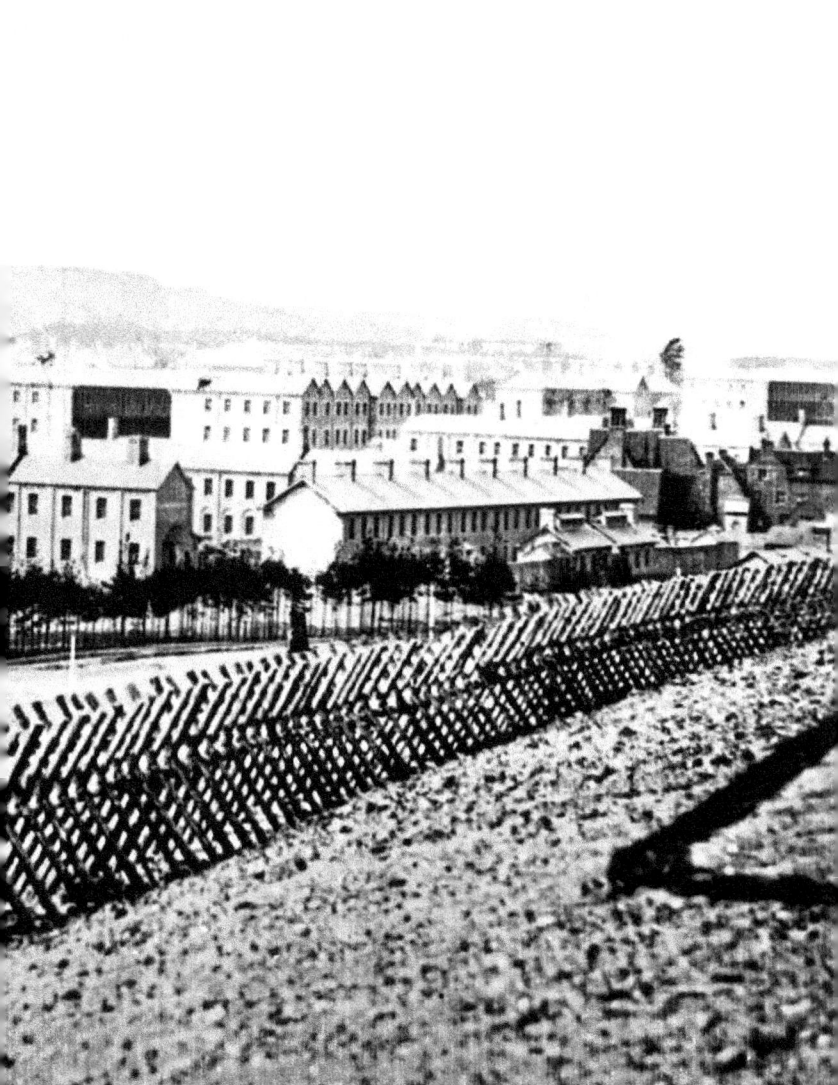

30. UNION BUILDING

The building dates from 1629 and was originally a sub-manor to the Tichborne mansion in Aldershot Park. In the early nineteenth century it became a workhouse for the poor and then by 1851 it was a school for pauper children. This picture from 1870 shows the Union Building after the Army took it over for a hospital. Later it was the Garrison Pay Office and then a families' centre, but now it has been converted into civilian apartments.

Walk down Hospital Hill and cross Wellington Avenue by the light-controlled crossing.

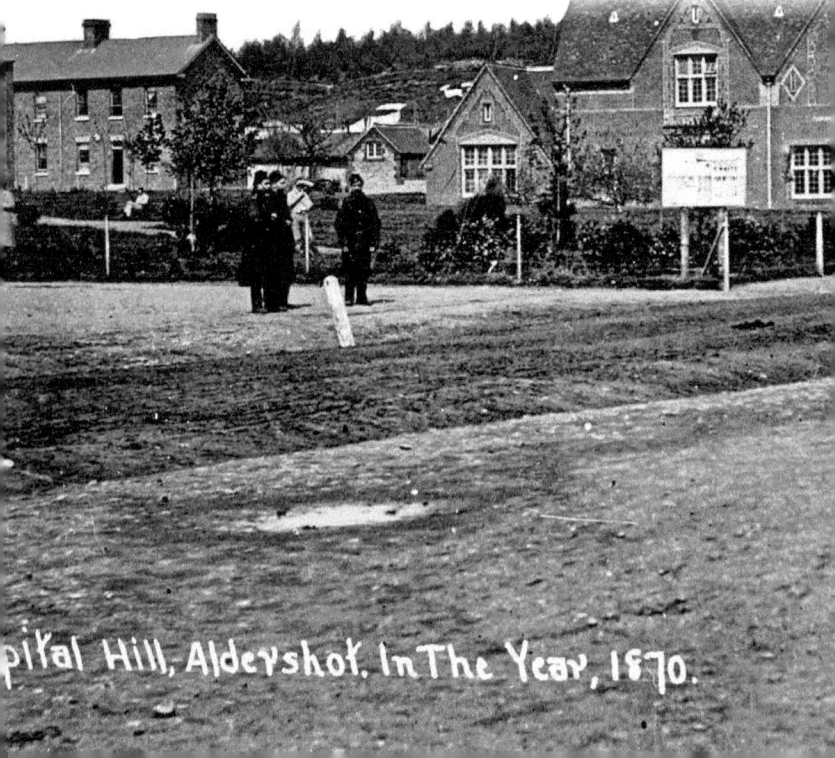

pital Hill, Aldershot. In The Year, 1870.

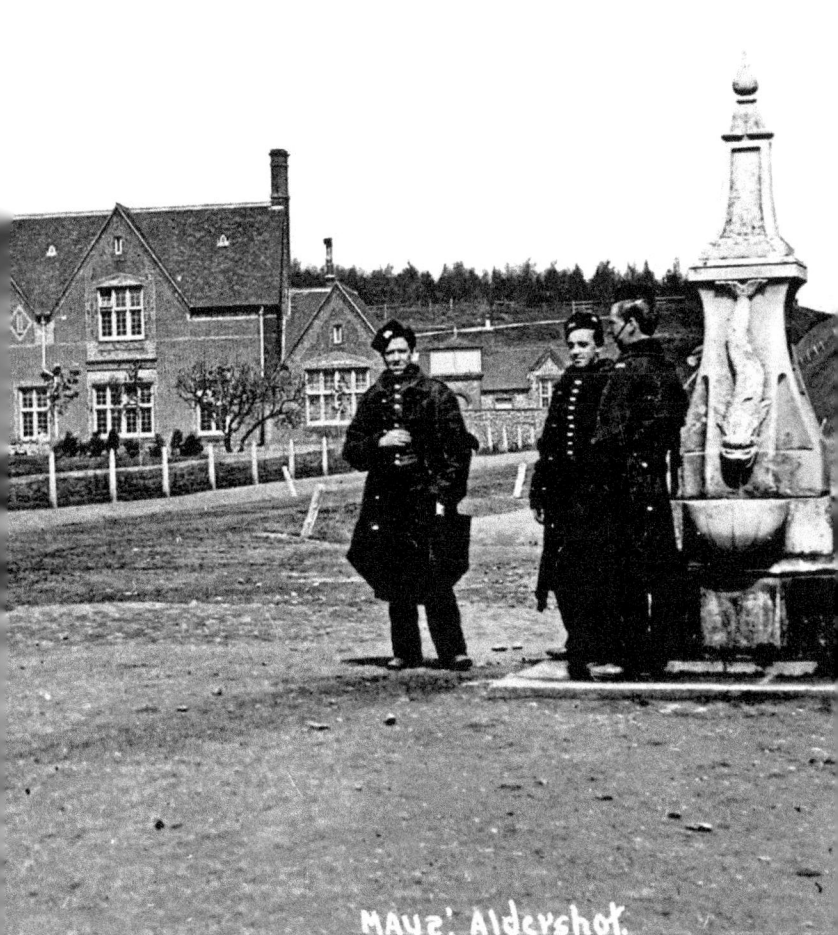

31. WARBURG CAVALRY BARRACKS

An interesting view of the buildings inside Warburg Barracks, where men of the 3rd Dragoon Guards are performing their 'Maypole' musical ride, *c.* 1910. After the demolition of Warburg in the 1960s, part of the area was used for the Princes Hall theatre and the police station, while the new Westgate covers the remainder of the site.

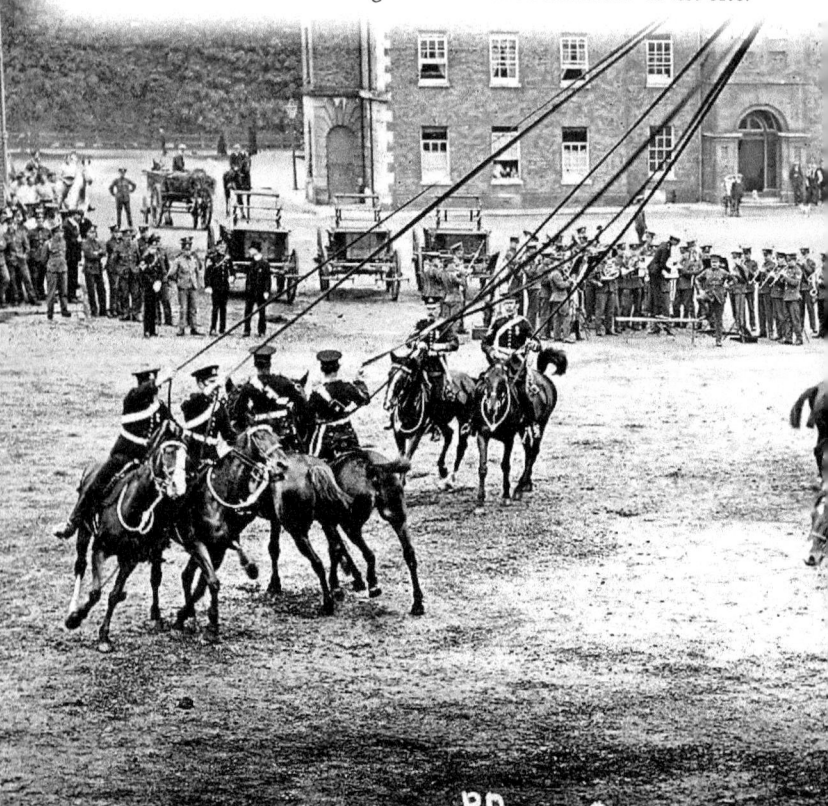

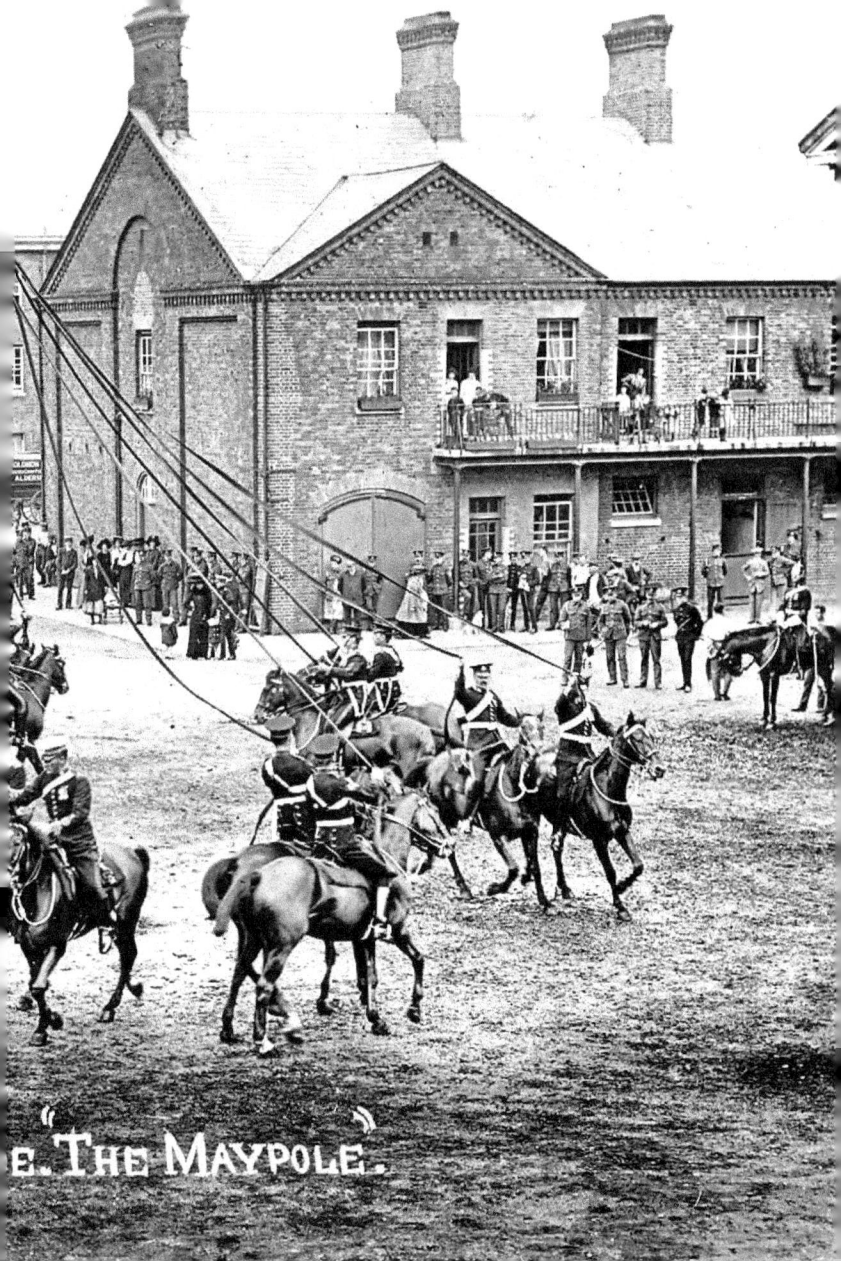
"THE MAYPOLE."

32. PRINCES GARDENS

The area that is now the Princes Gardens was where the Royal Engineers set up their base in late 1853 to survey the land for the camp; it remained the R. E. Yard until bought by the council in 1930 and laid out as gardens. This photograph from 1936 looks across to the old Talavera infantry barracks. A feature of Princes Gardens today is the modern bandstand, opened on 2 June 2012 to mark the queen's Diamond Jubilee.

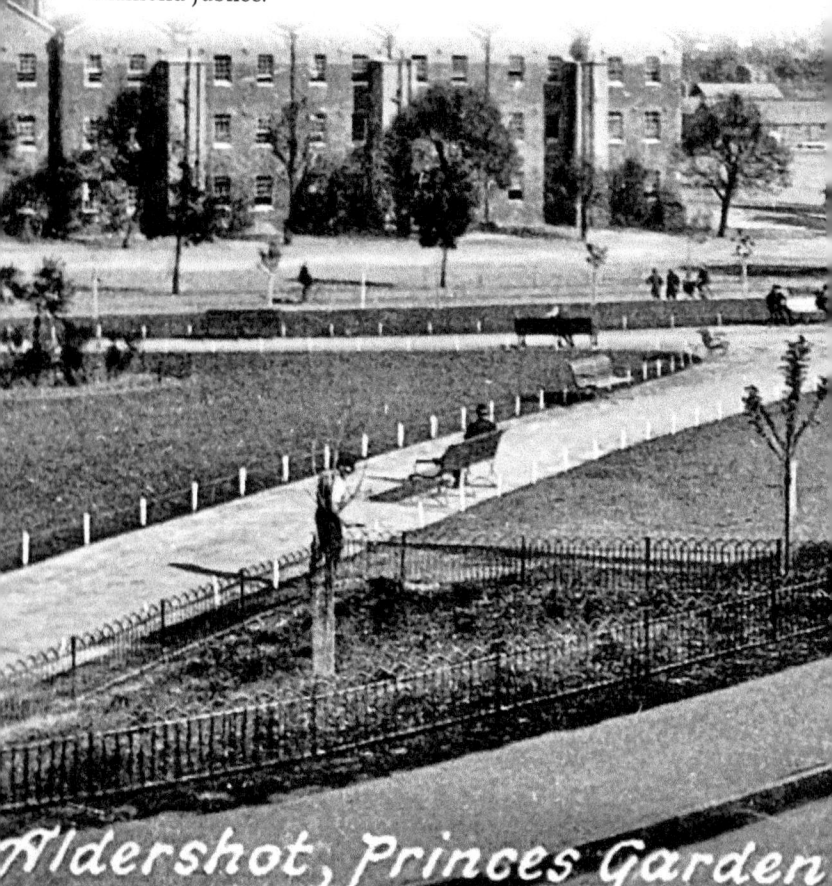

Aldershot, Princes Garden

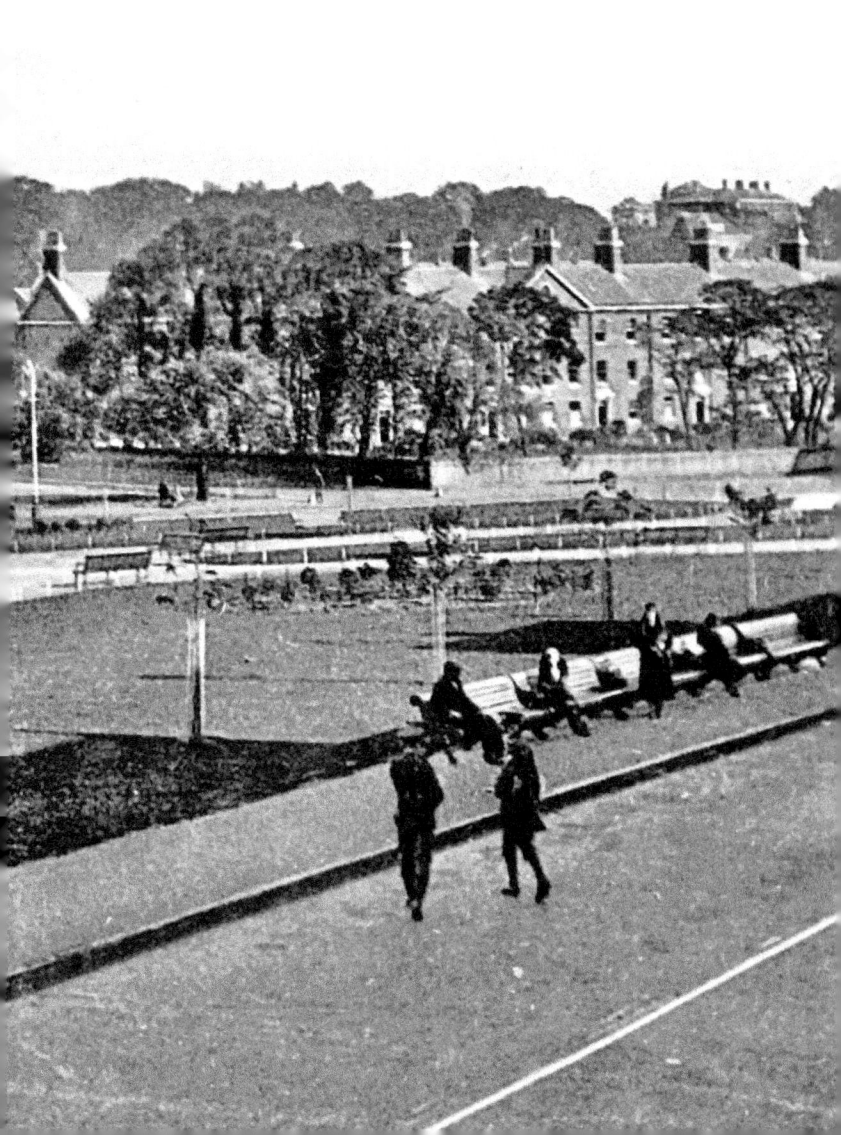

33. HIGH STREET FROM PRINCES GARDENS

This old photograph is around sixty years old, but little has changed in the view down the upper High Street. On the left are the Princes Gardens and the Empire and Ritz cinema buildings, although these are now respectively the Empire banqueting hall and restaurant and the Gala bingo hall. The buildings on the right are largely unchanged except for the shop windows and proprietors, and even the bus stops are in the same location.

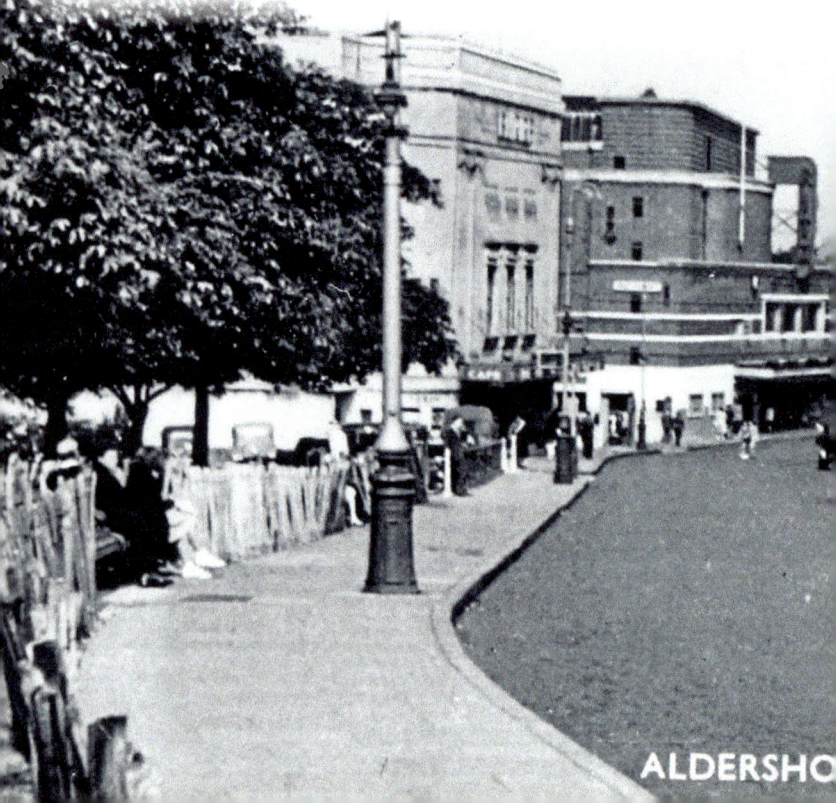

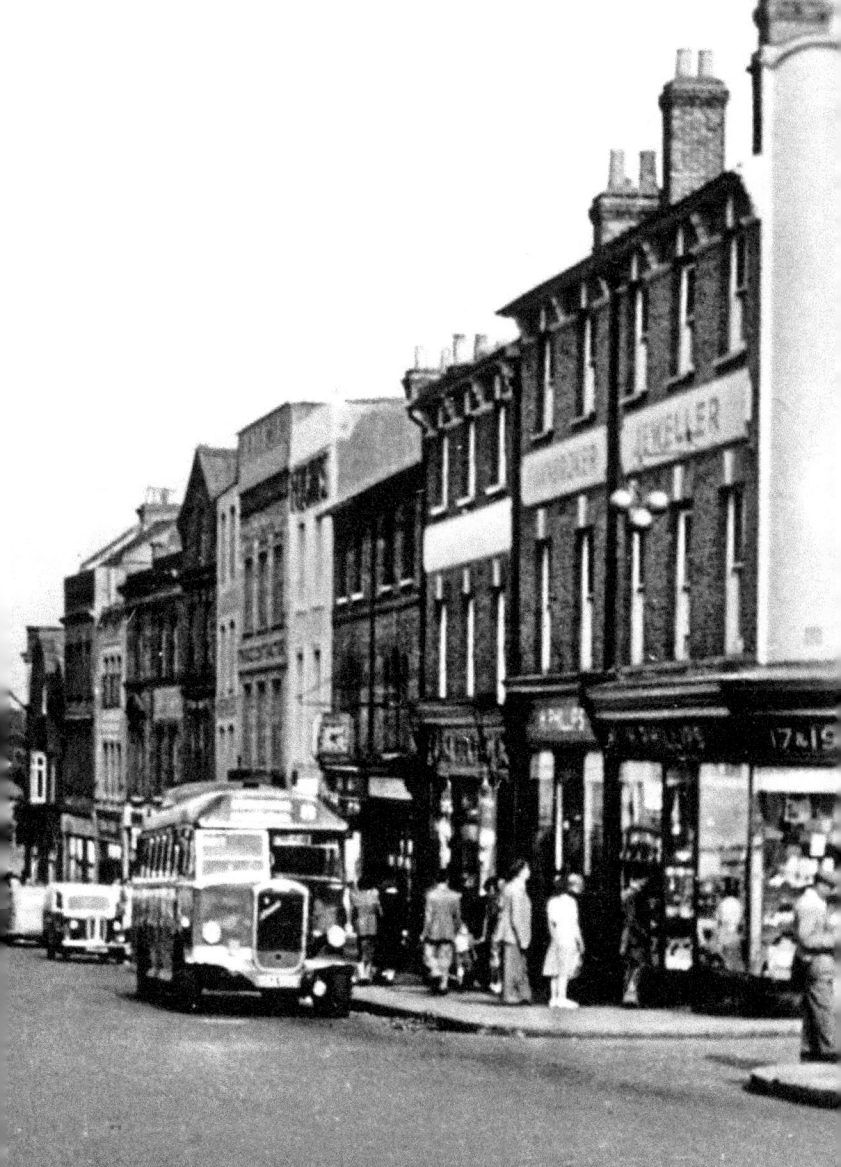

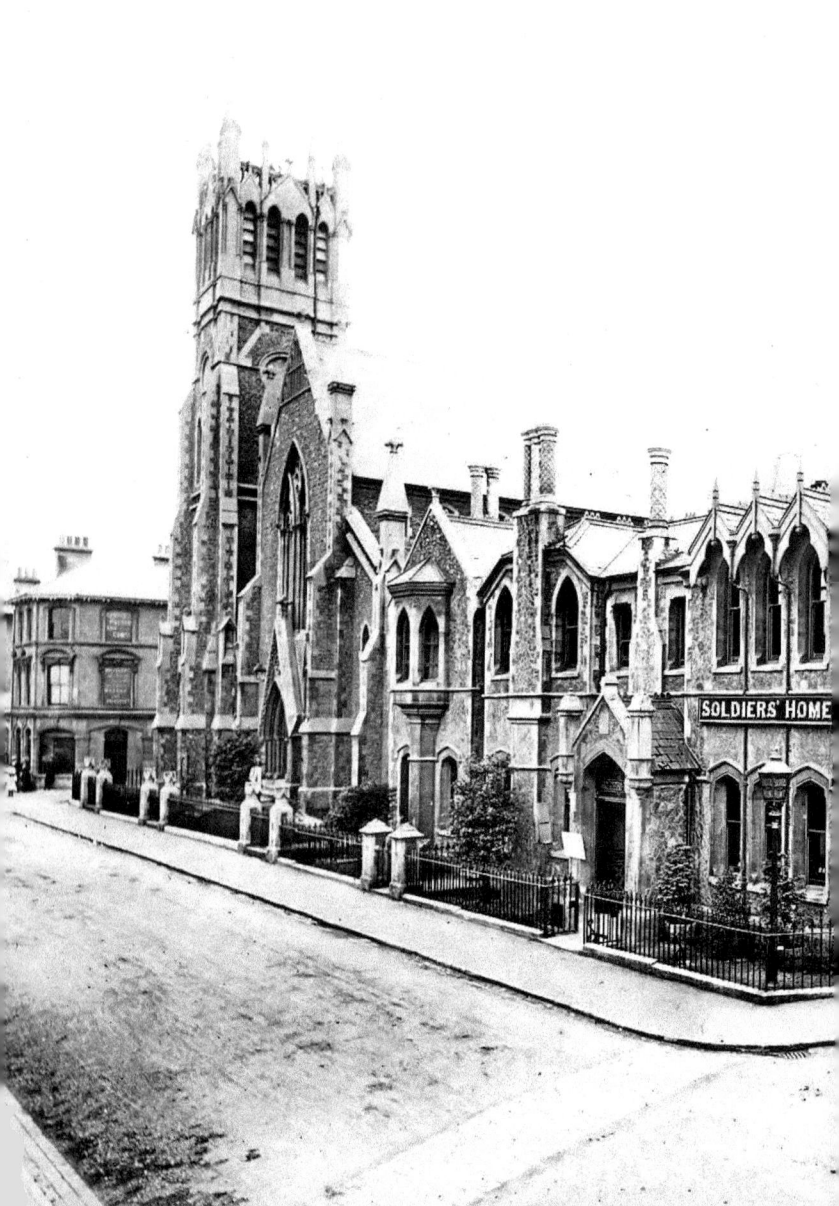

34. GROSVENOR ROAD SOLDIERS' HOME

Adjoining the Methodist church is the Grosvenor Road Soldiers' Home, shown in this early photograph from around 1905. The soldiers' home provided a comfortable environment in which troops could relax off duty, with reading rooms, games rooms, and refreshments. Today the soldiers' home has been converted into private residences.

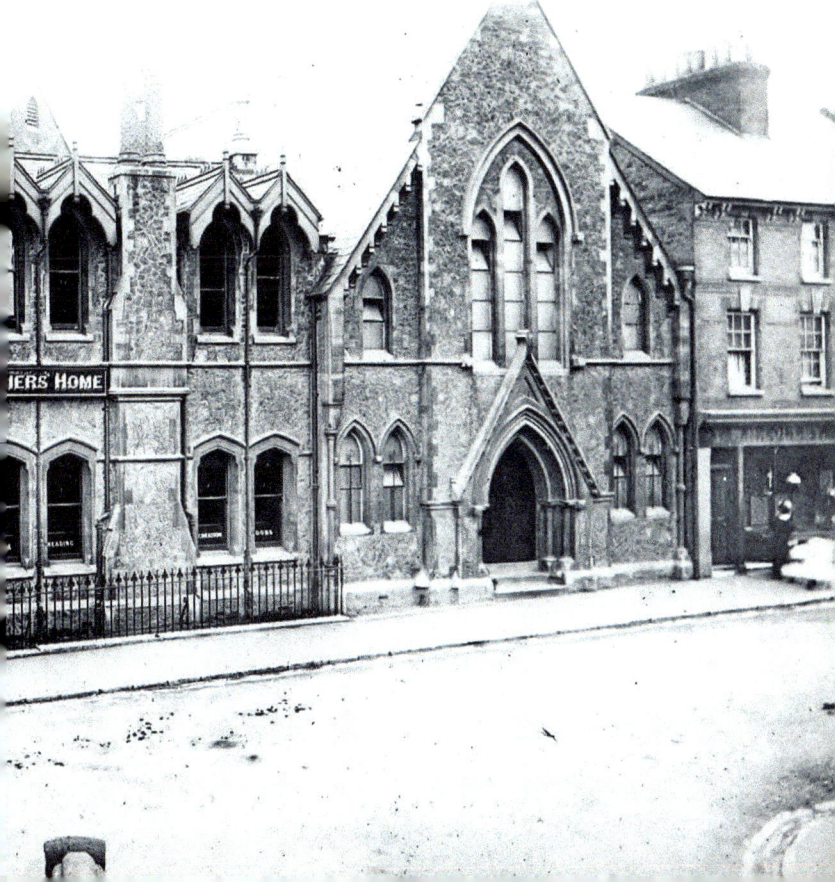

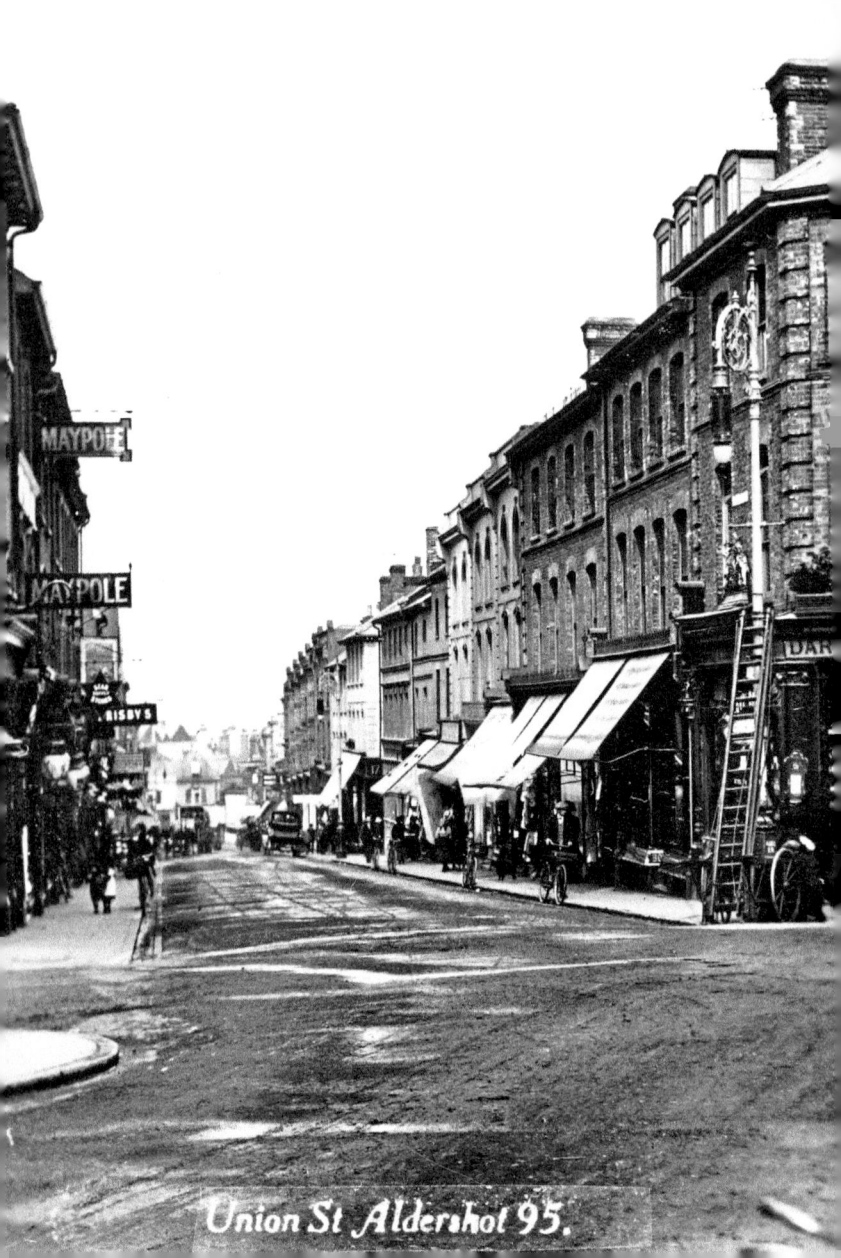

35. UNION STREET FROM GROSVENOR ROAD

The photograph looking down Union Street from Grosvenor Road in the 1920s provides an interesting contrast with the modern-day view. On the right in the old picture is Darracott's bakery, which was replaced by Court's furniture store, and which in turn has been replaced by residential flats. The road is now a pedestrian zone with modern planting and street furniture.

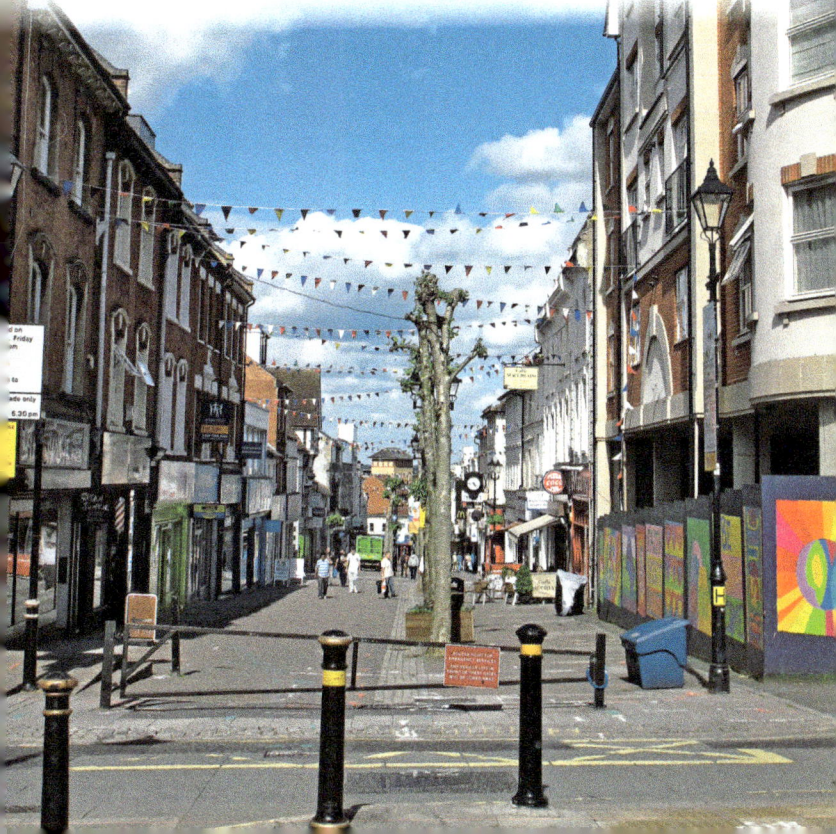

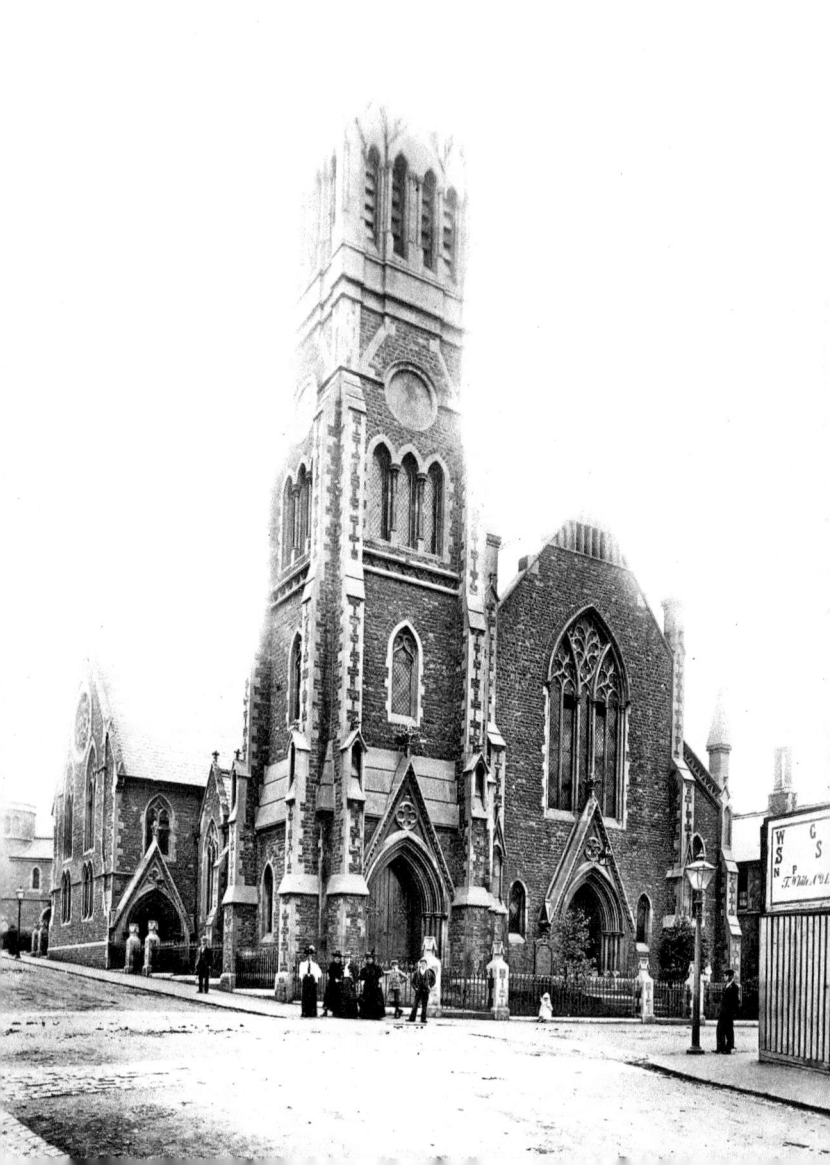

36. THE METHODIST CHURCH

The fine Methodist church on the corner of Grosvenor Road and Queen's Road was built in 1874 at a cost of £10,000, and its 100-feet-high tower is a local landmark. Although the building appears largely unchanged externally, it is no longer used for worship but for purposes as diverse as music studios, accountants' offices and a dental surgery. The conversion won the Rushmoor Civic Design Award in 1992, commemorated in the stone behind the sign.

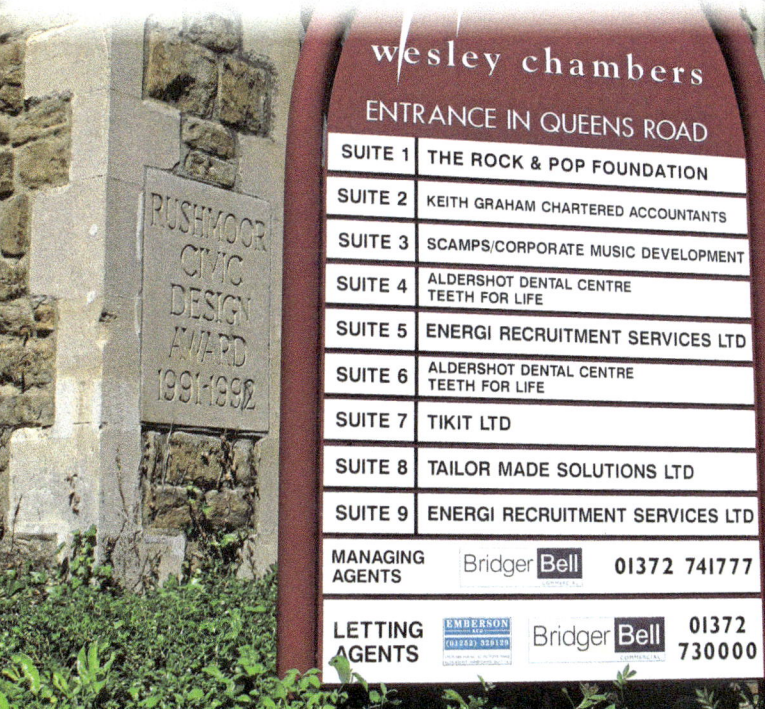

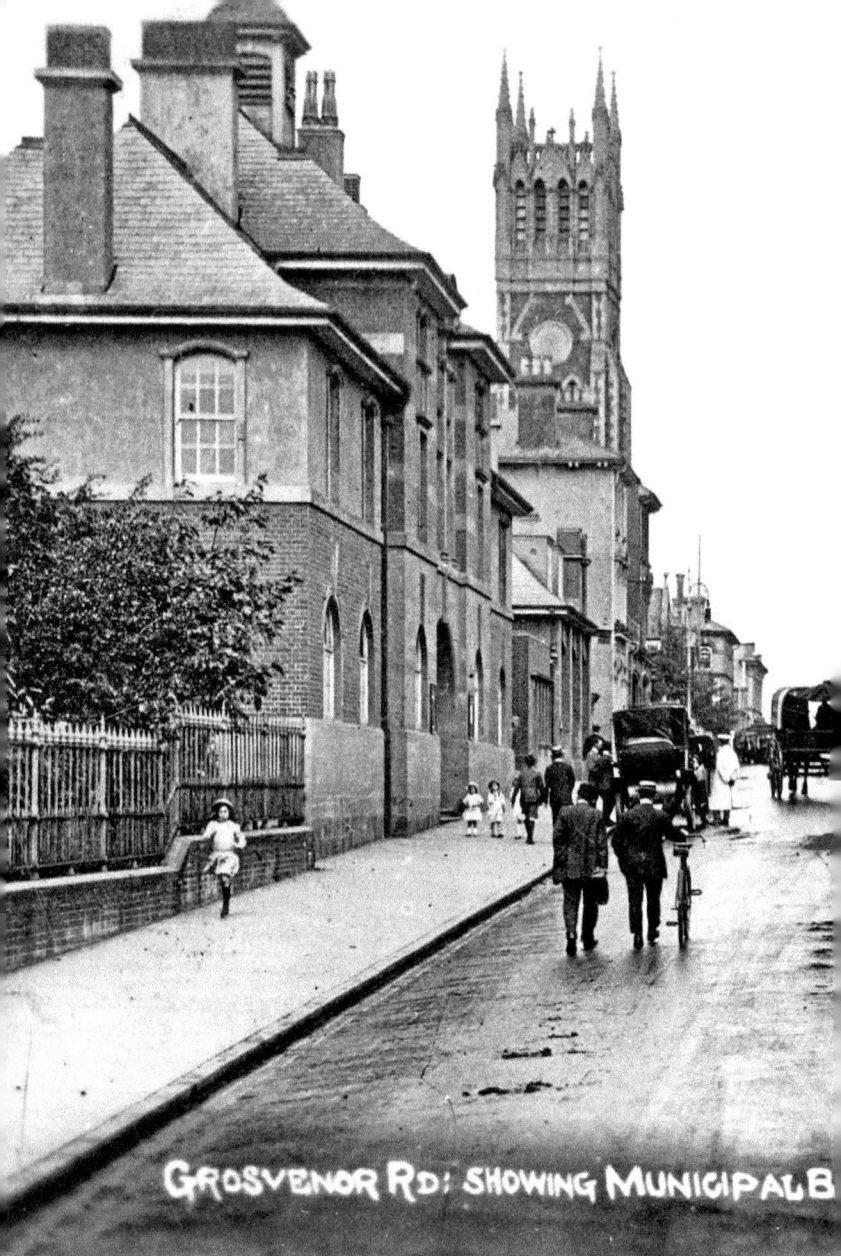

37. GROSVENOR ROAD

Looking north along Grosvenor Road around 1910, the right-hand side was mainly residential while on the left were the Municipal Gardens, the town hall (built in 1904), the fire station, and, in the distance, the Methodist church. The gardens, old town hall and church remain today, although the Victorian houses on the right have been replaced by modern homes.

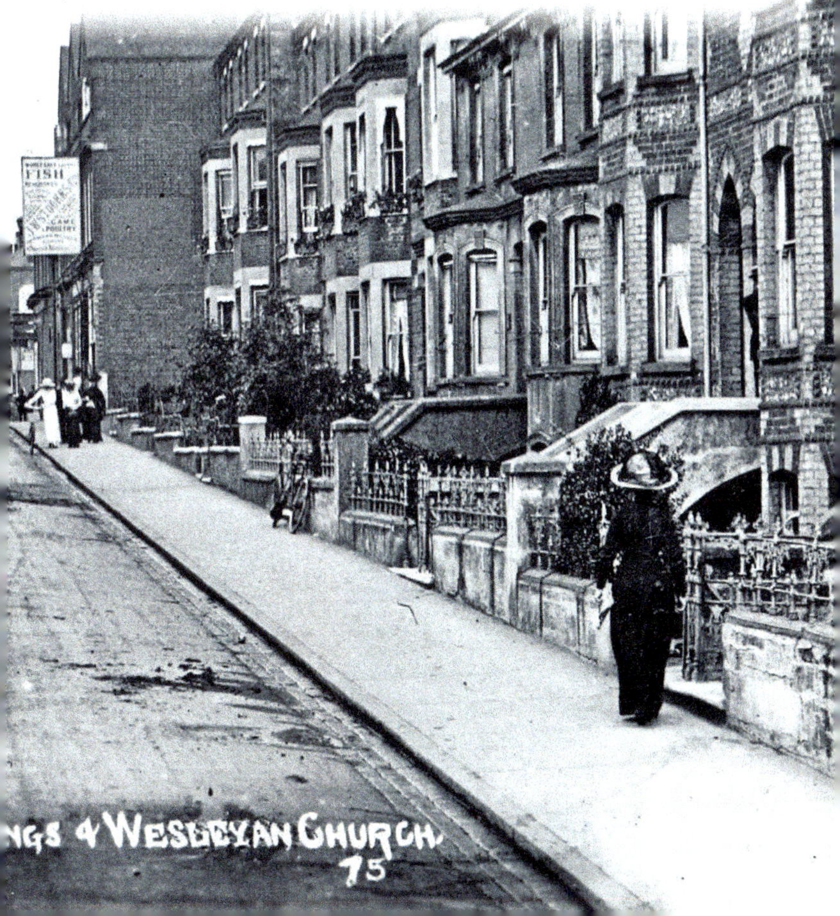

38. MUNICIPAL WAR MEMORIAL

The memorial to the people of Aldershot who lost their lives in the First World War was unveiled in the Municipal Gardens on 18 March 1925 by the Duke of Gloucester. In this old photograph from around 1927, the memorial is flanked by two captured field guns, one German and one Turkish, which were removed in the Second World War. In front of the memorial today is a fountain that was part of improvements to the gardens in 2000.

Retrace your steps back to the crossroads and turn right (east) into Victoria Road.

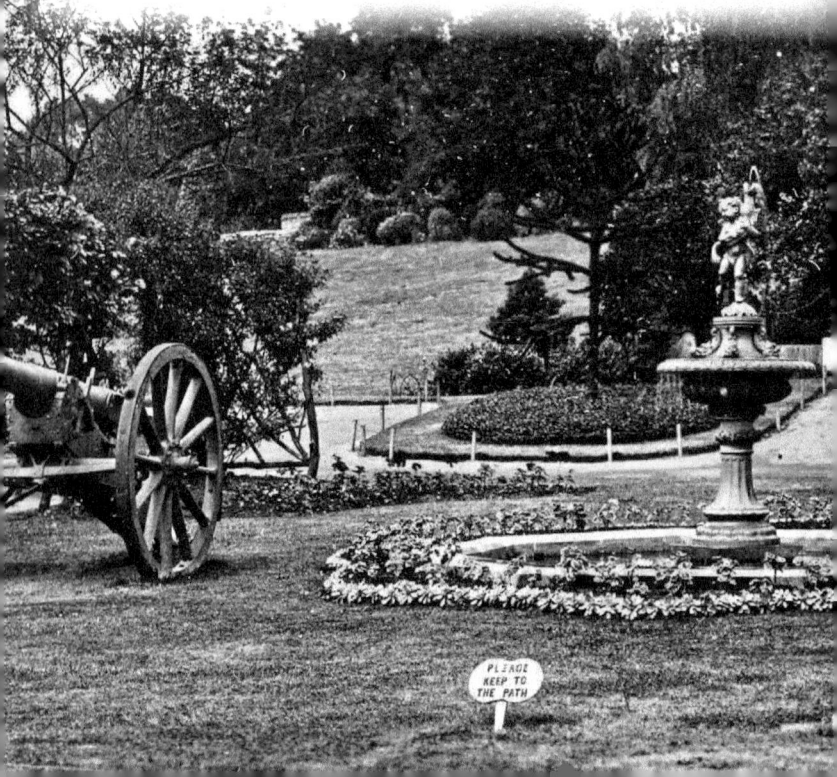

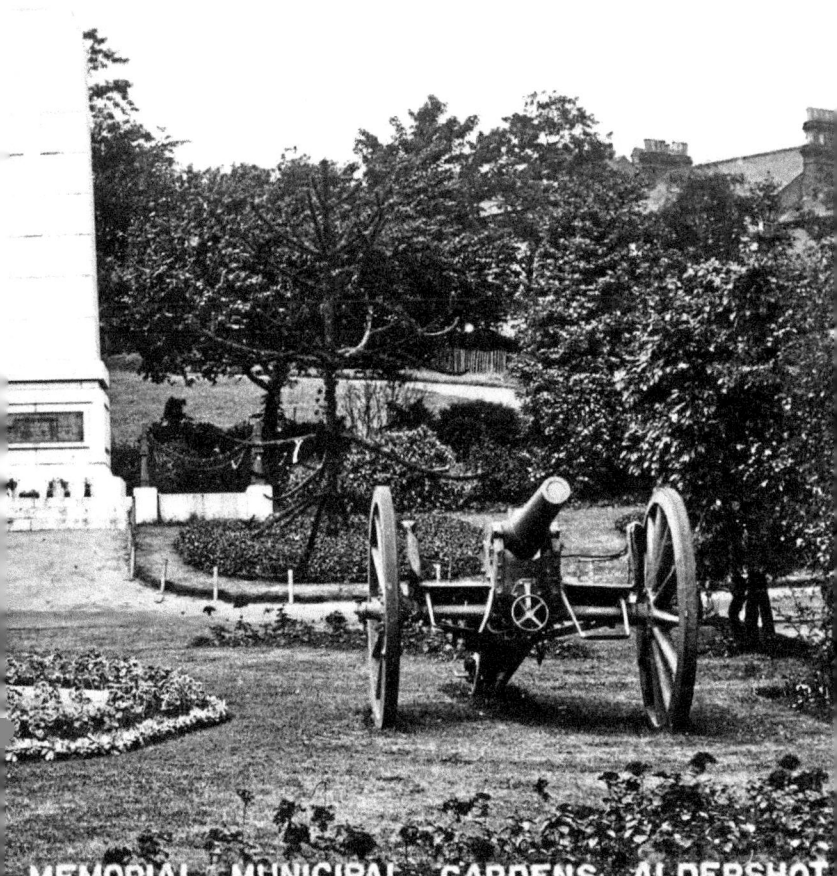

39. WELLINGTON STREET FROM VICTORIA ROAD

In the Edwardian view of Wellington Street the George Hotel is on the left and the London County and Westminster Bank on the right; beyond that are milliners Nelson and Goodrich and the entrance to the old arcade. Today the George is still a pub and the bank is the NatWest, but the old arcade has been demolished and the entrance blocked off by modern shops.

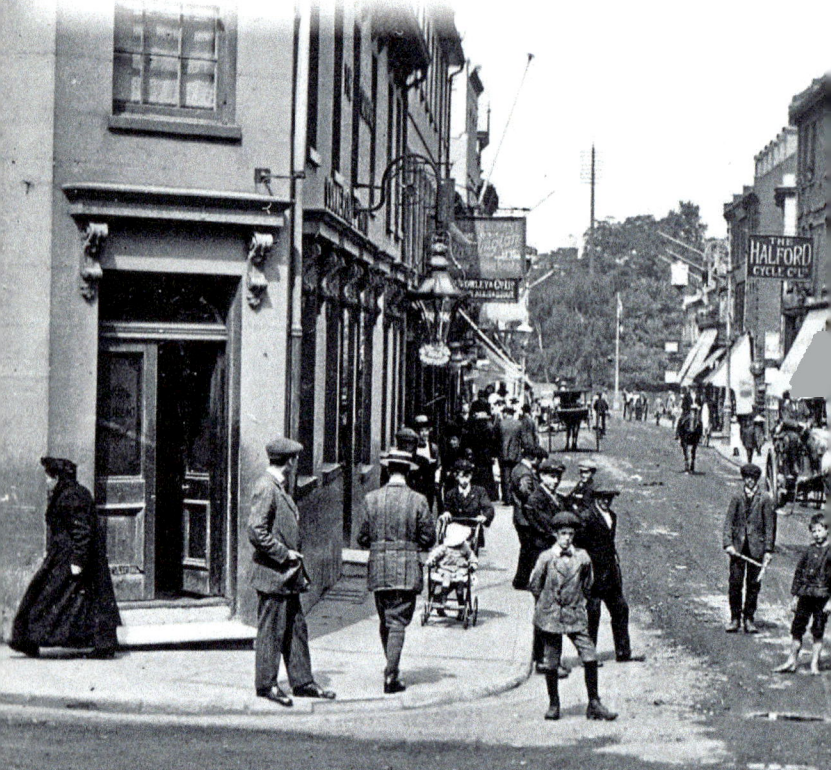

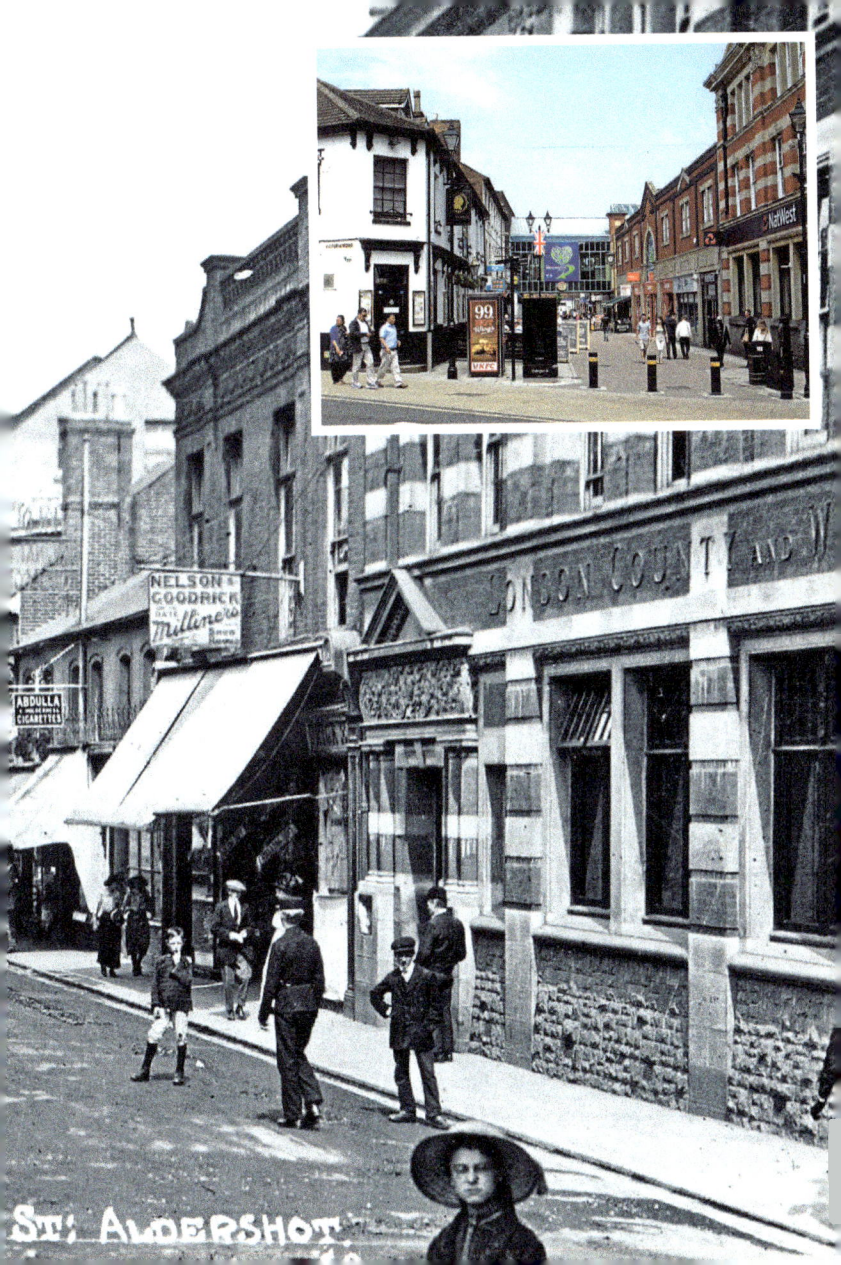

40. VICTORIA ROAD FROM THE POST OFFICE

Looking west up Victoria Road in 1909, the tower of the Methodist church can be seen in the distance, while on the right is the post office, built in 1902, and the Aldershot Institute, erected in 1887 by public subscription. Behind the trees on the left was the Church of England Soldiers' Institute. The view is still recognisable today, but the Soldiers' Institute has been replaced by a modern shop building.

Turn north into Station Road.

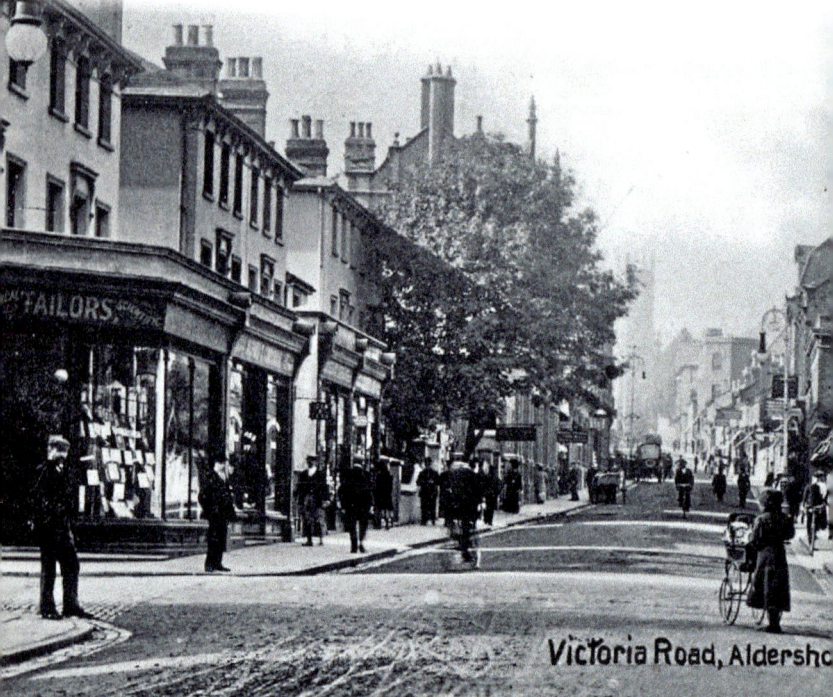

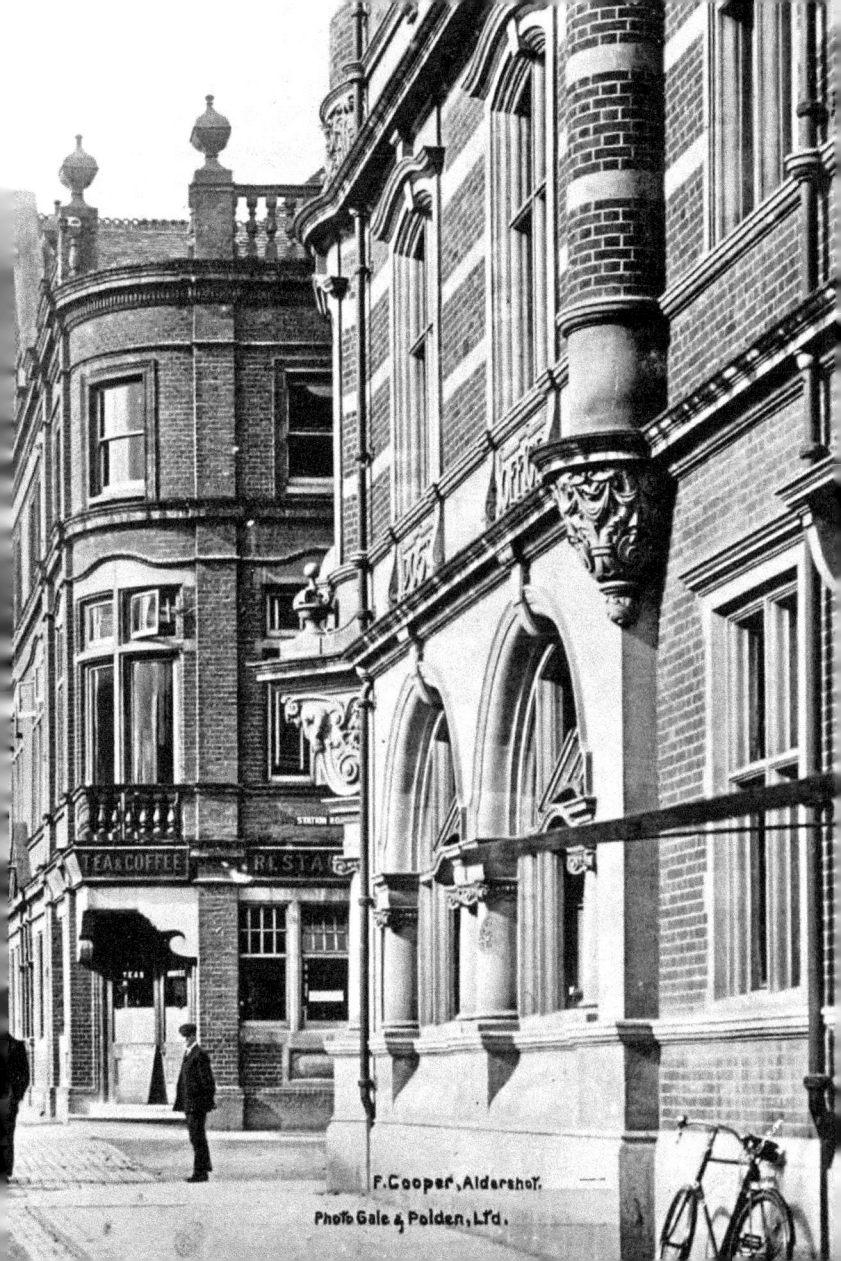

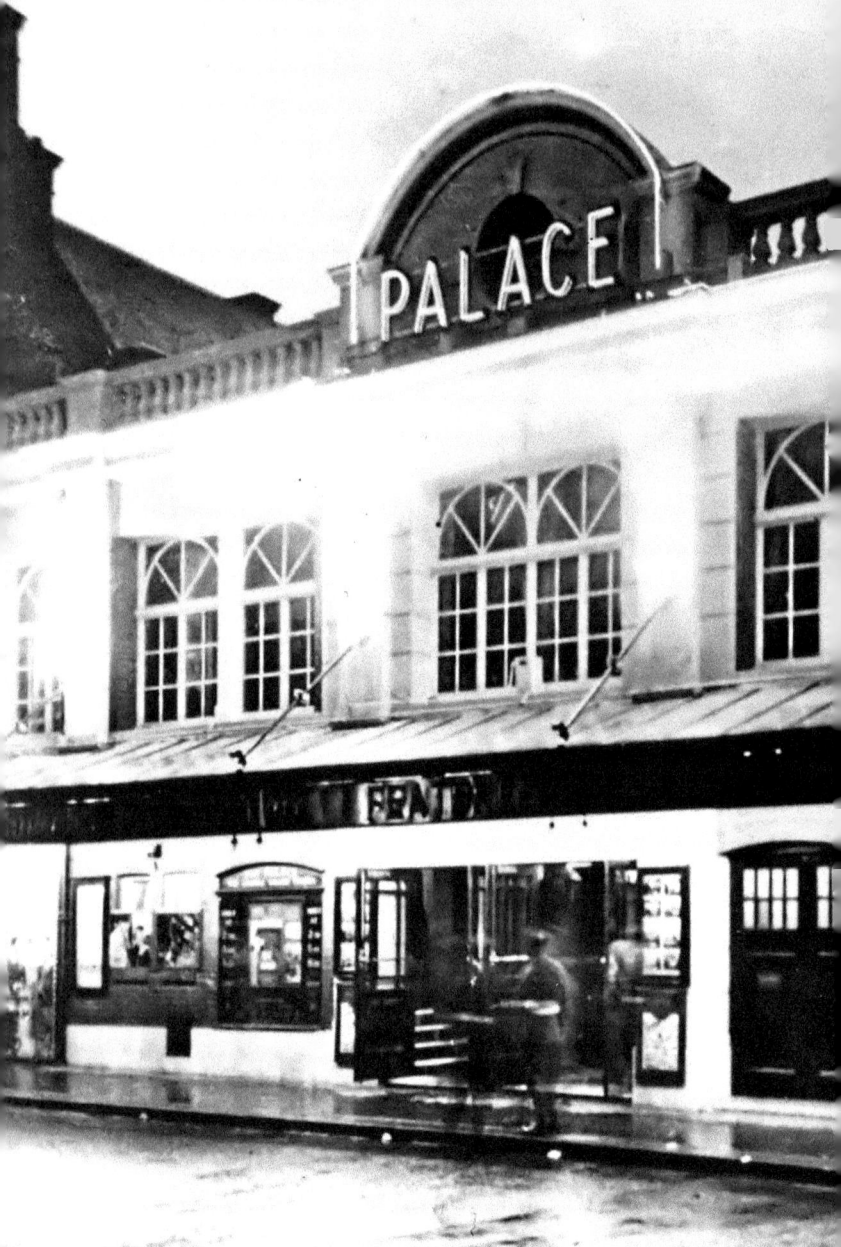

41. THE PALACE CINEMA

The Palace was the first purpose-built cinema in Aldershot and opened on Boxing Day 1912. The old photograph shows it ablaze with lights in its heyday around 1933. It closed as a cinema in 1985 and was turned into the Cheeks nightclub, then in 2010 it became a music venue with its original name of the Palace. This closed in 2011 and it was empty for some time, but now this Grade II-listed building has been reopened as an events venue.

Retrace your steps back to the crossroads, cross over Victoria Road at the traffic lights and continue south along Station Road.

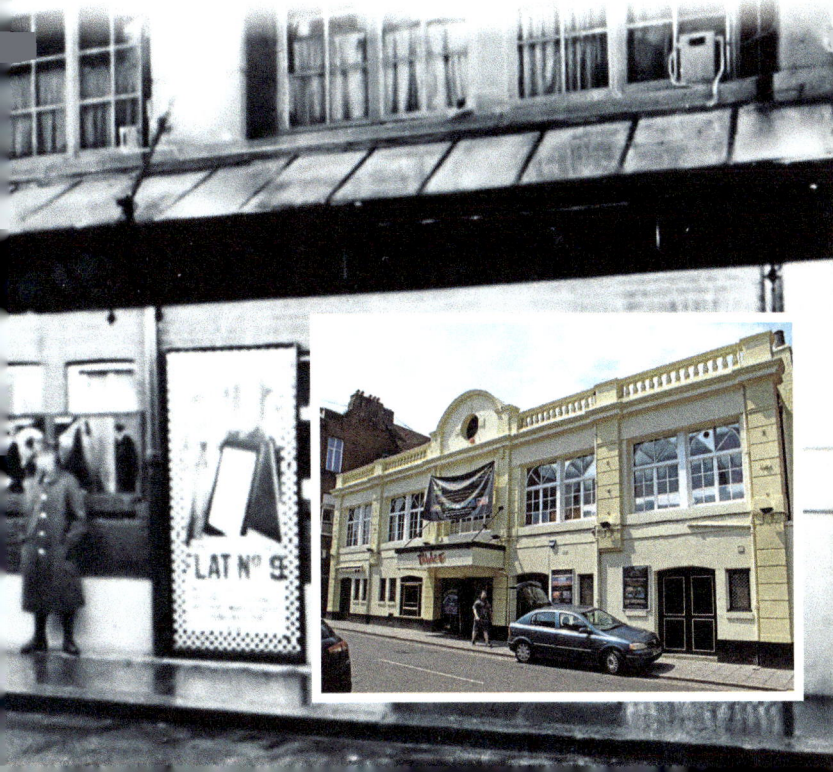

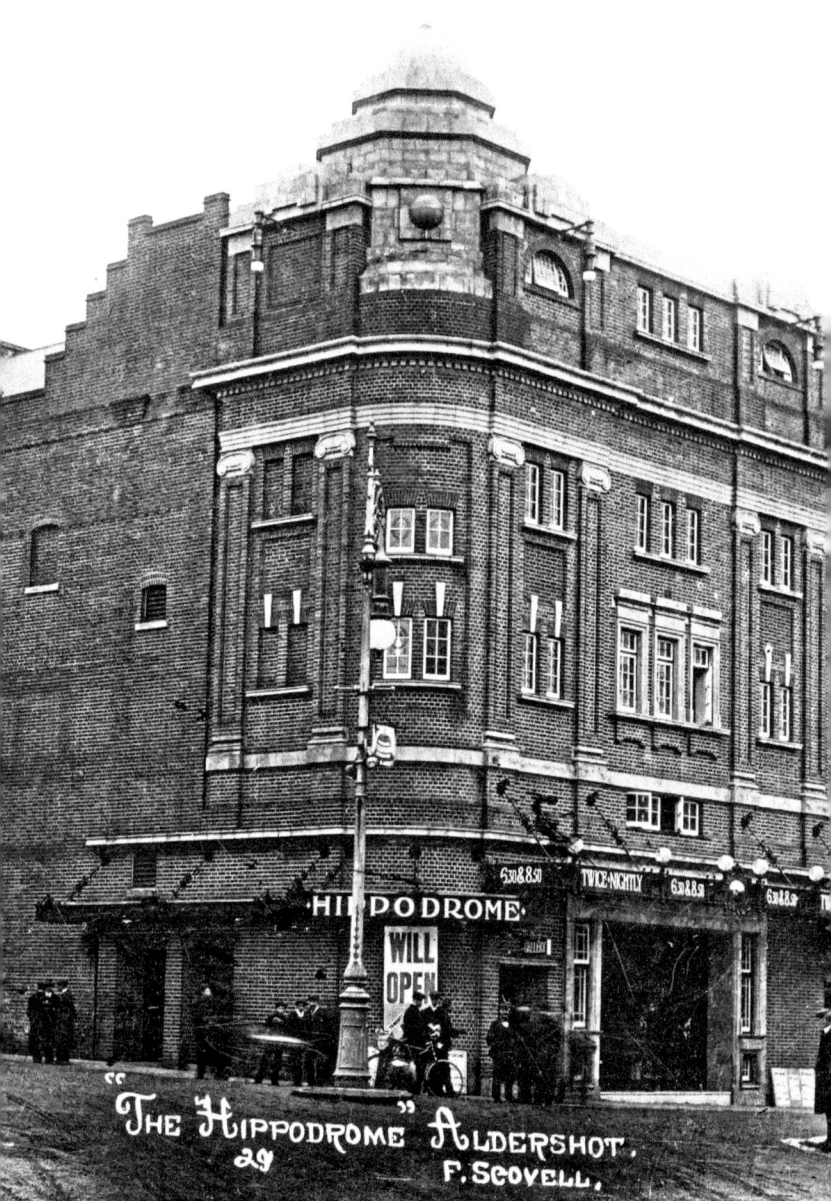

42. THE HIPPODROME

Aldershot's fine variety theatre, the Hippodrome, opened on 3 February 1913 on the corner of Station Road and Birchett Road. It was one of southern England's largest venues, able to seat up to 1,700, and was hugely popular during its fifty-year life. The theatre was demolished in 1962 and replaced by the dull and unimaginative Hippodrome House office block.

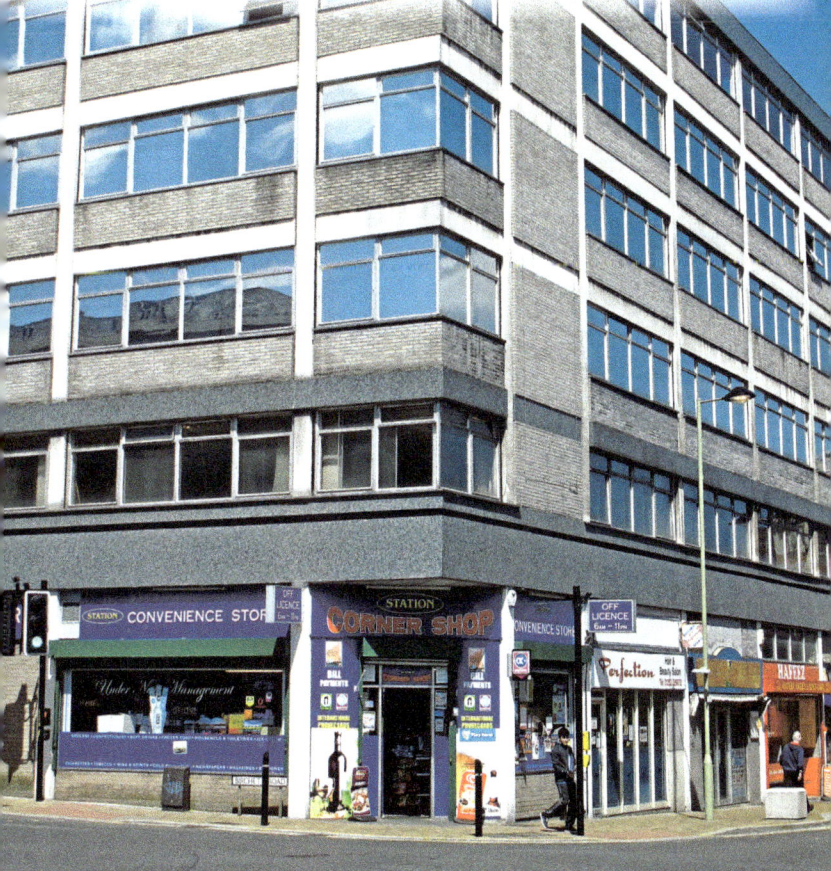

43. GALE AND POLDEN

Gale and Polden established their printing works in Aldershot in 1893 and it grew to be one of the town's largest businesses. There was a disastrous fire in 1918, and in the photograph men of the Aldershot volunteer fire brigade tackle the blaze. The firm was taken over by Robert Maxwell and closed in 1981. The site is now occupied by flats, but the design echoes the shape of the old printing works.

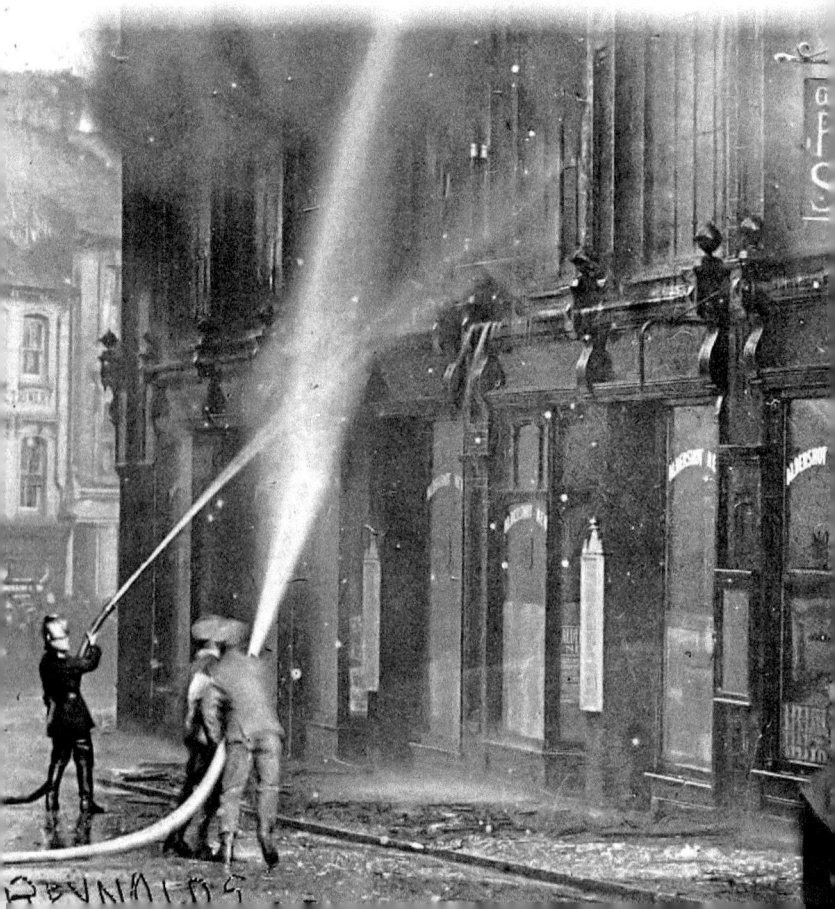

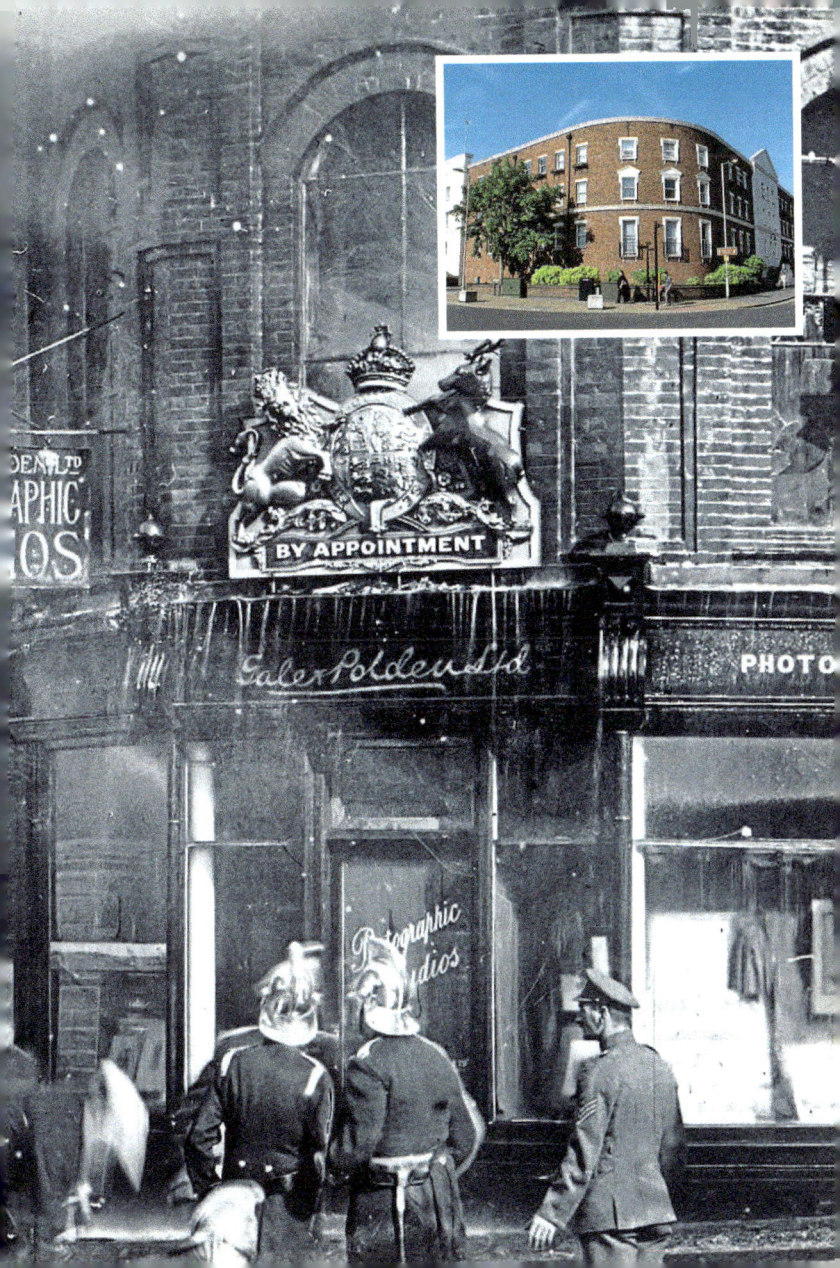

44. STATION ROAD AND THE SOUTH WESTERN HOTEL

In the view down Station Road from the 1930s, the Hippodrome variety theatre can be seen at the junction with Birchett Road, while in the foreground is the large South Western Hotel, built in 1867. Today, the theatre has been replaced by the Hippodrome House office block from the 1960s, while the South Western has been reduced to around a third of its original size and is now the Funky End bar.

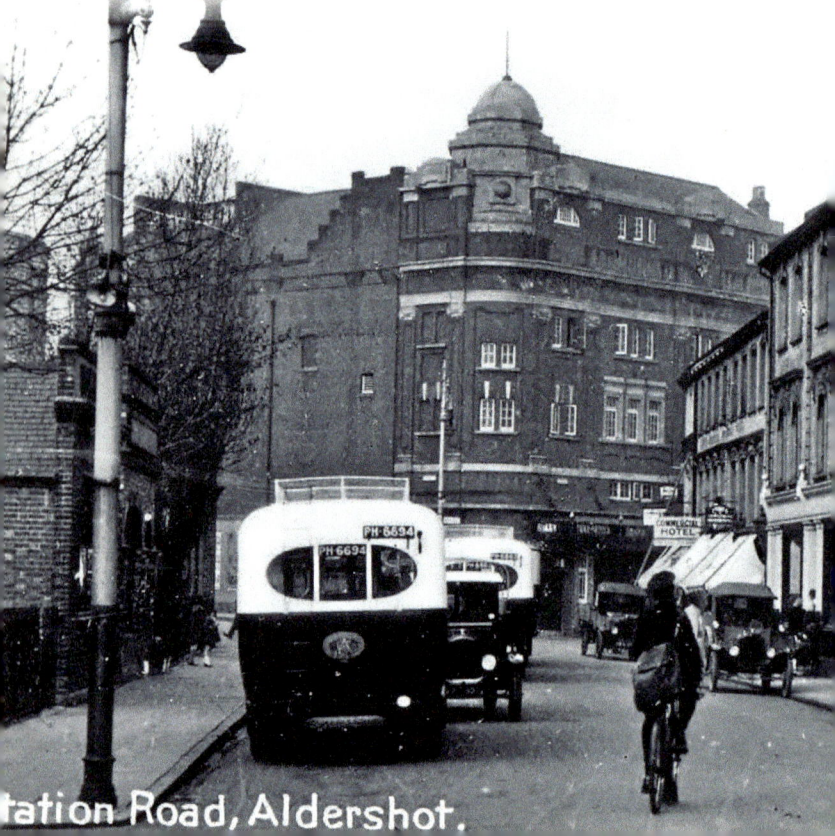

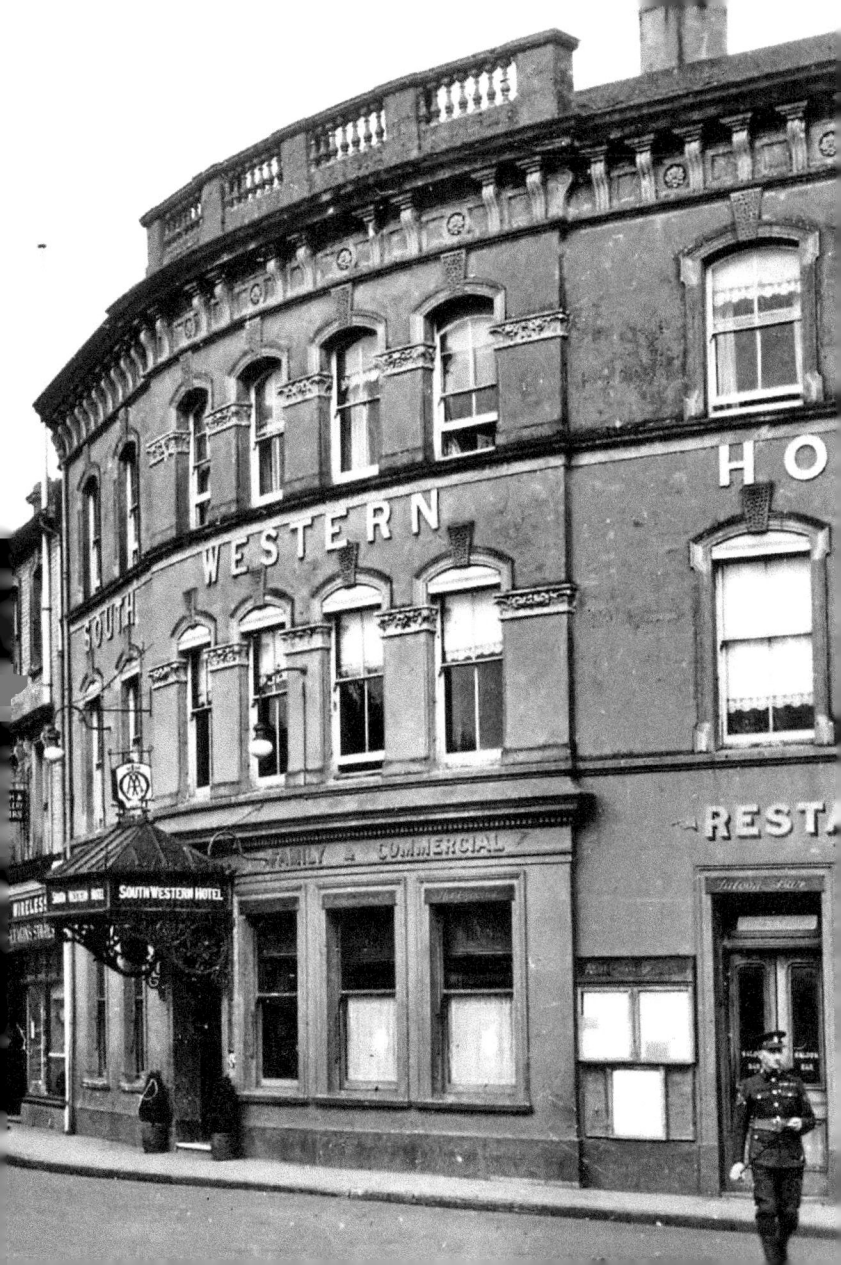

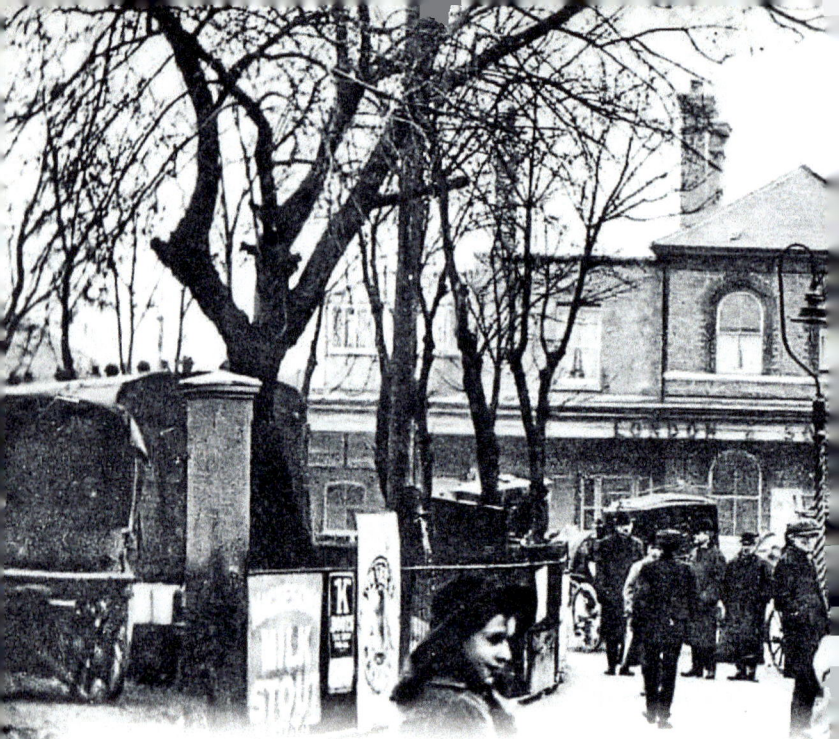

45. THE RAILWAY STATION APPROACH

When the camp was first established, the nearest railway station was Tongham, but with the rapid growth of the town a line was brought to Aldershot and the station was opened in 1870. This photograph from around 1910 shows lines of horse-drawn cabs waiting for passengers, and on the left is a carriage in the sidings. The station building remains in use today, but the sidings are now a car park and the taxis are motor powered.

To return to the starting point of the tour, cross over the footbridge, go down East Station Road to St Michael's Road, turn right and walk up to Manor Walk, which will take you along the top of Manor Park back to the parish church.

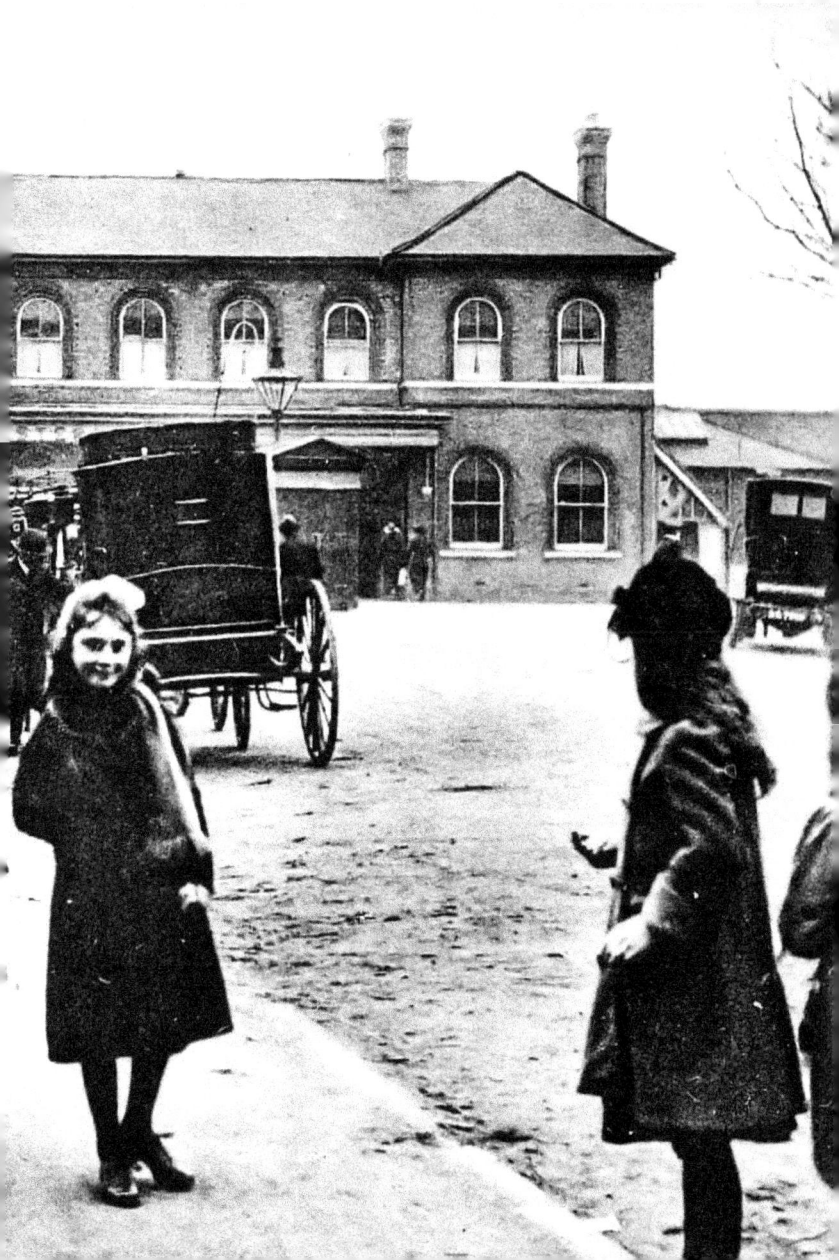

Also Available from Amberley Publishing

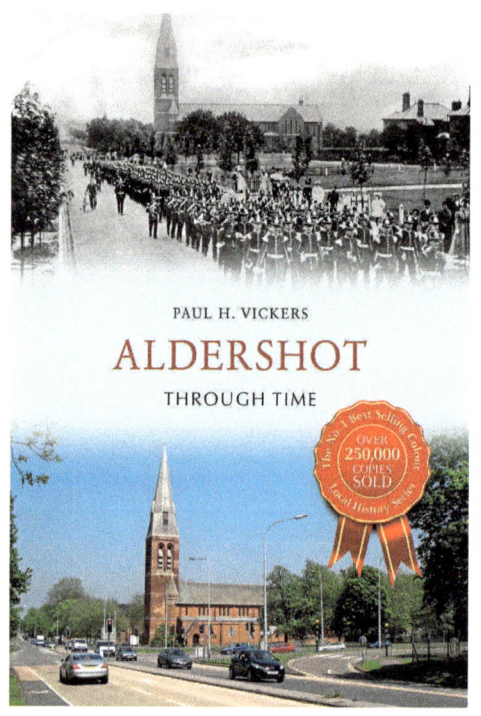

This fascinating selection of photographs traces some of the many ways in which Aldershot has changed and developed over the last century.

Paperback
180 illustrations
96 pages
978-1-4456-1026-9

Available from all good bookshops or to order direct
please call **01453-847-800**
www.amberley-books.com